Additional Practice
Workbook
GRADE 6

enVision® Mathematics

SAVVAS
LEARNING COMPANY

ISBN-13: 978-1-4182-6920-3
ISBN-10: 1-4182-6920-4

9 22

Grade 6
Topics 1–8

Topic 1   **Use Positive Rational Numbers**

Topic 2   **Integers and Rational Numbers**

Topic 3   **Numeric and Algebraic Expressions**

Topic 4   **Represent and Solve Equations and Inequalities**

Topic 5   Understand and Use Ratio and Rate

Topic 6   Understand and Use Percent

Topic 7   Solve Area, Surface Area, and Volume Problems

Topic 8   Display, Describe, and Summarize Data

1-1 Additional Practice

Scan for Multimedia

In 1–6, find each sum or difference.

1. 45.6 + 26.3

2. 14.25 − 5.14

3. 17.2 + 6.08

4. 3.652 − 1.41

5. 18.06 + 9.798

6. 8.006 − 6.38

In 7–9, find each product.

7. 4.89 × 2.2

8. 2.01 × 0.43

9. 54.1 × 0.69

10. Look for Relationships Complete the sequence of numbers in this set. Explain the pattern.

7.5   6.25   5

11. Critique Reasoning Jaime wrote 4.4 − 0.33 = 1.1. Is his answer reasonable? Explain why or why not.

12. The weights of 3 kittens at one week of age were 3.6 ounces, 4.2 ounces, and 3.3 ounces. If each kitten has gained 2.3 ounces, how much does each of the kittens weigh?

13. A movie theater is having a special. If a group of four pays $7.25 each for tickets, each person can get popcorn and a drink for $5.75. Use the expression 4(5.75 + 7.25) to find the total cost for 4 friends.

14. Reasoning If you multiply two decimals that are less than 1, can you predict whether the product will be less than or greater than either of the factors? Explain.

15. Two factors are multiplied and their product is 34.44. One factor is a whole number. What is the least number of decimal places in the other factor? Explain.

16. Make Sense and Persevere A factory makes parts for toys in different quantities, as shown in the table. How much would 11 parts cost?

Number of Parts	2	7	12	15
Cost	$0.90	$3.15	$5.40	$6.75

17. The perimeter of a 5-sided figure is 45.56 meters. Two of the sides have the same length. The sum of the other three side lengths is 24.2 meters. How long is each of the same-length sides? Explain.

18. Critique Reasoning Kim multiplied 8×0.952 and got 76.16. How can you estimate to show that Kim's answer is incorrect?

19. Higher Order Thinking The decimal 104.3 becomes 1,043 when multiplied by 10. The same number becomes 10.43 when multiplied by 0.10. Explain why.

☑ Assessment Practice

20. Use the information in the table to solve each problem.

Craft Supplies	
Poster board	$1.29/sheet
Markers	$4.50/pack
Tape	$1.99/roll
Glue	$2.39/tube
Construction paper	$3.79/pack

PART A

How much more does 1 tube of glue cost than 1 roll of tape?

PART B

What is the total cost for 2 packs of markers and a pack of construction paper?

Name: _____

1-2 Additional Practice

Scan for
Multimedia

In 1–4, divide. Record remainders.

1. $13\overline{)1{,}722}$

2. $44\overline{)6{,}668}$

3. $48\overline{)4{,}896}$

4. $65\overline{)99{,}521}$

In 5–8, divide. Write remainders as decimals.

5. $34 \div 10$

6. $9 \div 90$

7. $231 \div 42$

8. $9{,}751 \div 98$

In 9–12, divide.

9. $78.32 \div 2$

10. $14.36 \div 4$

11. $66.15 \div 5$

12. $8.2 \div 2$

In 13–16, divide. Annex zeros if needed to write remainders as decimals.

13. $188.4 \div 60$

14. $0.86 \div 0.004$

15. $59.6 \div 8$

16. $11.2 \div 25$

17. Vicky makes jewelry. She uses 42 beads for each necklace that she makes, and she has 500 beads. How many necklaces can she make? Explain.

18. **Critique Reasoning** Dana said that $0.6 \div 30 = 0.02$. Is she correct? Explain.

In 19–21, use the diagram at the right.

Samantha visits her local farmer's market to buy apples and oranges to make a fruit salad. She has $10.00 to spend.

19. If Samantha buys only apples, how many can she buy?

20. If Samantha buys only oranges, how many can she buy?

21. Samantha decides to buy both apples and oranges. Give two different solutions to tell how many apples and how many oranges she might buy.

Oranges
$0.38 each

Apples
$0.26 each

22. **Construct Arguments** April has 905 baseball cards. She wants to organize them on pages that hold 18 cards each. She has 50 pages. Does April have enough pages to organize all her cards? Explain.

23. **Higher Order Thinking** How do you know that $1.016 \div 4.064 \neq 0.025$ without doing the division?

24. **Make Sense and Persevere** You have $15.60 to buy juice boxes. Each juice box costs $0.80. How many juice boxes can you buy? Should you expect to get change when you pay for the juice boxes? If so, how much?

25. When you divide 7.7 by 700, how many decimal places will the quotient have? Use place-value reasoning to explain how you know.

26. Which bag of potatoes costs more per pound? How much more?

Potatoes	
12-pound bag	$6.96
25-pound bag	$15.75

☑ Assessment Practice

27. What is the value of the expression 1,408 ÷ 27?

Ⓐ 52

Ⓑ 52 R 4

Ⓒ 52.14

Ⓓ 52 R 14

28. Which expression has the same solution as 2,640 ÷ 12?

Ⓐ 2,873 ÷ 13

Ⓑ 3,080 ÷ 14

Ⓒ 3,314 ÷ 15

Ⓓ 3,526 ÷ 16

1-3 Additional Practice

Scan for
Multimedia

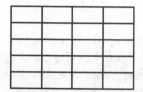

In 1–3, find each product. Shade the model to help solve.

1. $\frac{4}{7} \times \frac{2}{3}$

2. $\frac{1}{2} \times \frac{11}{12}$

3. $\frac{2}{5} \times \frac{1}{4}$

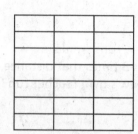
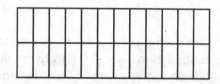

In 4–7, find each product.

4. $\frac{3}{4} \times \frac{1}{8}$

5. $\frac{8}{9} \times \frac{9}{10}$

6. $\frac{3}{7} \times \frac{2}{3}$

7. $\frac{1}{5} \times \frac{5}{6}$

In 8–11, estimate the product. Then find each product.

8. $4 \times 6\frac{1}{4}$

9. $3\frac{2}{3} \times 2\frac{3}{4}$

10. $\frac{7}{8} \times 4\frac{1}{6}$

11. $1\frac{1}{2} \times 2\frac{3}{4}$

In 12 and 13, use the diagram at the right.

12. Keyshia is riding her bike on Bay View Bike Path. Keyshia's bike got a flat tire $\frac{2}{3}$ of the way down the path, so she had to stop. How far did Keyshia ride?

Bay View Bike Path $\frac{7}{8}$ mile

13. The Cityscape Bike Path is $2\frac{2}{3}$ times longer than the Bay View Bike Path. What is the length of the Cityscape Bike Path?

14. Vincent found a recipe for banana macadamia nut bread that uses $\frac{3}{4}$ cup of macadamia nuts. If he wants to make only half of the recipe, how many cups of macadamia nuts should Vincent use?

15. **Higher Order Thinking** If $\frac{1}{2}$ is multiplied by $\frac{1}{2}$, will the product be greater than $\frac{1}{2}$? Explain.

16. Of the apps on Juan's tablet, $\frac{3}{4}$ are gaming apps, and $\frac{5}{7}$ of the gaming apps are action games. What fraction of the apps on Juan's tablet are action games?

17. In gym class, Matthew runs $\frac{3}{4}$ mile. His gym teacher runs 3 times that distance. How far does Matthew's gym teacher run?

18. Patrick walks $\frac{9}{10}$ mile to the gym. How far has he walked when he has covered $\frac{2}{3}$ of the distance to the gym?

19. **Construct Arguments** Which is greater, $\frac{4}{7} \times \frac{1}{4}$ or $\frac{4}{7} \times \frac{1}{6}$? Explain.

20. One World Trade Center in New York City is about $3\frac{1}{5}$ times as tall as the Washington Monument in Washington, D.C. The Washington Monument is 555 feet tall. About how tall is One World Trade Center?

21. **Reasoning** Lucie can walk about $3\frac{4}{5}$ miles each hour. About how far can she walk in 2 hours 45 minutes?

22. **Be Precise** The stained glass window shown is a regular hexagon. How can you use multiplication to find the window's perimeter?

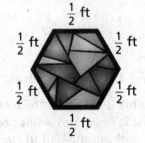

$\frac{1}{2}$ ft

$\frac{1}{2}$ ft $\frac{1}{2}$ ft

$\frac{1}{2}$ ft $\frac{1}{2}$ ft

$\frac{1}{2}$ ft

Assessment Practice

23. Which of these equations is equivalent to $6\frac{3}{4} \times 3\frac{1}{4} = 19$?

    Ⓐ $3\frac{1}{4} \div 19 = 6\frac{3}{4}$

    Ⓑ $19 \div 3\frac{1}{4} = 6\frac{3}{4}$

    Ⓒ $3\frac{1}{4} \div 6\frac{3}{4} = 19$

    Ⓓ $6\frac{3}{4} \div 3\frac{1}{4} = 19$

24. Which of these equations is equivalent to $\frac{2}{3} \times 3\frac{1}{4} = 2\frac{1}{6}$? Select all that apply.

    ☐ $2\frac{1}{6} \div 3\frac{1}{4} = \frac{2}{3}$

    ☐ $2\frac{1}{6} \div \frac{2}{3} = 3\frac{1}{4}$

    ☐ $\frac{2}{3} \div 3\frac{1}{4} = 2\frac{1}{6}$

    ☐ $3\frac{1}{4} \div \frac{2}{3} = 2\frac{1}{6}$

    ☐ $\frac{2}{3} \div 2\frac{1}{6} = 3\frac{1}{4}$

1-4 Additional Practice

In 1 and 2, complete each division sentence.

1. $\frac{2}{3} \div \boxed{} = \frac{1}{3}$

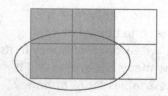

2. $3 \div \boxed{} = 5$

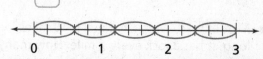

In 3 and 4, find each quotient. Draw a diagram to help.

3. $\frac{3}{5} \div 2$

4. $4 \div \frac{2}{5}$

In 5–8, find each reciprocal.

5. $\frac{5}{9}$

6. 8

7. $\frac{7}{3}$

8. $\frac{1}{12}$

In 9–16, find each quotient.

9. $8 \div \frac{2}{5}$

10. $4 \div \frac{1}{6}$

11. $18 \div \frac{3}{8}$

12. $\frac{4}{5} \div 4$

13. $20 \div \frac{3}{4}$

14. $9 \div \frac{1}{8}$

15. $15 \div \frac{1}{3}$

16. $6 \div \frac{2}{3}$

17. **Reasoning** A store sells honey in $\frac{3}{8}$-quart jars. If the store has 24 quarts of honey available on a shelf, how many jars of honey are on the shelf?

18. **Higher Order Thinking** Olivia divided a fraction by $\frac{3}{4}$. The quotient was a whole number. Was the dividend less than $\frac{3}{4}$? Explain.

19. A construction worker has a rope that is 10 meters long. She needs to cut it into pieces that are each $\frac{2}{9}$ meter long. How many pieces can she cut without having any rope left over?

20. Some friends are making cakes for a bake sale. They need 6 cups of sugar. However, they only have a $\frac{1}{4}$-cup measuring cup. How many times will they need to fill the measuring cup?

21. Model with Math A canal is 10 miles long. It has a lock every $\frac{2}{3}$ mile. How many locks are on the canal? Draw a number line to represent the problem.

22. Make Sense and Persevere It is estimated that one honeybee can make about $\frac{1}{12}$ teaspoon of honey in its lifetime. How many honeybees will it take to make 2 tablespoons of honey? One tablespoon is equivalent to 3 teaspoons.

23. A recording of the current weather conditions lasts $\frac{3}{4}$ minute. If the recording plays repeatedly, how many times would it play in 1 hour?

24. How many $\frac{3}{8}$-pound burgers can be made from 3 pounds of ground turkey?

25. Model with Math A team is practicing on a $\frac{3}{8}$-acre field. The coach divides the field into two equal parts for the practice. What fraction of an acre is each part? Use the rectangle to represent the problem. Then write an equation to show the solution.

The rectangle represents 1 whole acre. Draw lines to represent $\frac{3}{8}$ acre first. Then divide that into 2 equal parts.

Assessment Practice

26. Select all the math statements that have the same solution.

- $8 \div \frac{2}{3} = \frac{8}{1} \times \frac{3}{2}$
- $20 \div \frac{5}{4} = 20 \times \frac{4}{5}$
- $12 \div \frac{3}{4} = 12 \times \frac{4}{3}$
- $28 \div \frac{7}{4} = 28 \times \frac{4}{7}$
- $16 \div \frac{4}{5} = 16 \times \frac{5}{4}$

27. Select all the math statements that are true.

- $\frac{1}{4} \div 4 = \frac{1}{4} \div \frac{4}{1} = \frac{1}{4} \times \frac{1}{4}$
- $\frac{2}{5} \div 5 = \frac{2}{5} \div \frac{5}{1} = \frac{2}{5} \times \frac{1}{5}$
- $\frac{4}{8} \div 8 = \frac{4}{8} \div \frac{1}{8} = \frac{4}{8} \times \frac{8}{1}$
- $\frac{2}{4} \div 4 = \frac{2}{4} \div \frac{4}{1} = \frac{2}{4} \times \frac{1}{4}$
- $\frac{2}{7} \div 6 = \frac{2}{7} \div \frac{1}{6} = \frac{2}{7} \times \frac{6}{1}$

1-5 Additional Practice

Scan for Multimedia

In 1–4, complete each division sentence using the models provided.

1. $\dfrac{3}{4} \div \dfrac{1}{12} = \boxed{}$

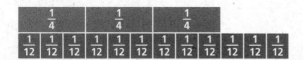

2. $\dfrac{4}{5} \div \dfrac{1}{10} = \boxed{}$

3. $\dfrac{5}{6} \div \dfrac{1}{6} = \boxed{}$

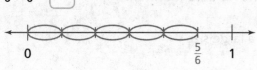

4. $\dfrac{3}{5} \div \dfrac{1}{10} = \boxed{}$

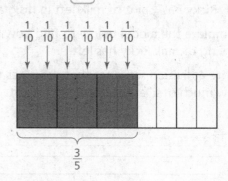

In 5–16, find each quotient.

5. $\dfrac{7}{8} \div \dfrac{1}{8}$

6. $\dfrac{6}{7} \div \dfrac{2}{7}$

7. $\dfrac{3}{4} \div \dfrac{1}{16}$

8. $\dfrac{5}{8} \div \dfrac{5}{16}$

9. $\dfrac{3}{4} \div \dfrac{5}{6}$

10. $\dfrac{9}{10} \div \dfrac{4}{5}$

11. $\dfrac{1}{3} \div \dfrac{3}{8}$

12. $\dfrac{4}{7} \div \dfrac{3}{4}$

13. $\dfrac{11}{12} \div \dfrac{2}{3}$

14. $\dfrac{8}{9} \div \dfrac{3}{4}$

15. $\dfrac{1}{4} \div \dfrac{6}{7}$

16. $\dfrac{1}{7} \div \dfrac{1}{5}$

17. **Be Precise** Brenda makes wooden coasters. She cuts small round posts into $\dfrac{2}{3}$-inch-thick disks of wood. How many coasters can Brenda make from a post that measures $\dfrac{1}{2}$ foot in length?

18. **Higher Order Thinking** When will the quotient of two fractions that are less than 1 be greater than either fraction?

19. Model with Math Juice glasses used at the Good Morning Restaurant hold $\frac{1}{8}$ quart of juice. A small pitcher holds $\frac{3}{4}$ quart of juice.

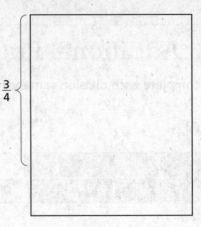

a. Complete the model at the right to find how many juice glasses can be filled from one small pitcher.

b. Write a division sentence that describes the model and tells how many juice glasses can be filled.

20. Model with Math A large-size serving of milk at the restaurant contains $\frac{3}{4}$ pint. Ricky has $\frac{1}{2}$ pint of milk left in his glass.

a. Complete the model below to find how much of a large-size serving of milk Ricky has left.

b. Write a division sentence that describes the model and tells how much of a large-size serving is left.

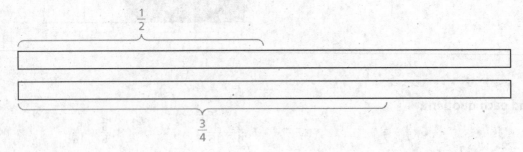

21. Write a problem that can be solved by dividing $\frac{9}{10}$ by $\frac{1}{4}$.

22. A student incorrectly claims that $\frac{2}{3} \div \frac{5}{9} = \frac{5}{6}$. Find the correct quotient. What was the student's error?

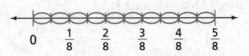

23. Which division sentence is shown by the model at the right?

Ⓐ $10 \div \frac{1}{16} = 160$

Ⓑ $10 \div \frac{5}{8} = 16$

Ⓒ $\frac{5}{8} \div \frac{1}{16} = 10$

Ⓓ $\frac{5}{8} \div \frac{1}{10} = 6\frac{1}{4}$

1-6 Additional Practice

In 1–12, find each quotient.

1. $2\frac{2}{3} \div 3\frac{1}{4}$

2. $17 \div 3\frac{2}{5}$

3. $2\frac{1}{5} \div 2\frac{1}{3}$

4. $5\frac{1}{4} \div 3$

5. $28 \div 4\frac{2}{3}$

6. $3\frac{1}{2} \div 2\frac{1}{4}$

7. $3\frac{3}{4} \div 2$

8. $1\frac{1}{2} \div 2\frac{1}{4}$

9. $2\frac{3}{8} \div 8\frac{9}{10}$

10. $8\frac{4}{5} \div 1\frac{1}{4}$

11. $8 \div 1\frac{1}{3}$

12. $5\frac{1}{7} \div 3$

13. On a recent trip, Jeremy and Frank drove 790 miles on $33\frac{1}{3}$ gallons of gas. How many miles per gallon did their car get on this trip?

14. Otto put $12\frac{4}{9}$ pounds of electrical supplies into crates. Each crate held $1\frac{7}{9}$ pounds of supplies. How many crates did Otto use?

15. Peggy practices her gymnastics routine for a total of 21 hours. Each practice session is $1\frac{3}{4}$ hours. How many practice sessions does Peggy have?

16. Hillary pours 10 cups of orange juice into glasses that hold $1\frac{2}{3}$ cup each. How many glasses does Hillary fill?

In 17–19, use the table at the right.

17. How many kitchens can Max paint with 20 gallons?

18. How many living rooms can Max paint with 26 gallons?

19. How many bedrooms can Max paint with 60 gallons?

Gallons of Paint Max Needs for Each Room

Room	Gallons of Paint
Kitchen	$2\frac{1}{2}$
Bedroom	$3\frac{3}{4}$
Living room	$4\frac{1}{3}$

20. A wheat farmer has a storage bin that holds $6,846\frac{1}{4}$ cubic feet. If a bushel of wheat fills $1\frac{1}{4}$ cubic feet, how many bushels can the storage bin hold?

21. **Higher Order Thinking** Without dividing, how can you decide which quotient is greater: $5\frac{1}{4} \div 3\frac{1}{2}$ or $5\frac{1}{4} \div 2\frac{1}{2}$?

22. Geraldo has a gold chain that is 34 inches long. He cuts it into $2\frac{1}{8}$-inch-long chains. How many gold chains does Geraldo have now?

23. Carl writes $\frac{14}{3} \times \frac{7}{3}$ to find the quotient of $4\frac{2}{3} \div 2\frac{1}{3}$. What is his mistake?

Assessment Practice

24. Franco has decorating ribbon that is $18\frac{3}{4}$ feet long, to be used for gift packages.

PART A

Each package requires $2\frac{1}{2}$ feet of ribbon. Which solution shows how many packages Franco can decorate with his ribbon?

Ⓐ 46 packages; $18\frac{3}{4} \times 2\frac{1}{2}$

Ⓑ $\frac{2}{15}$ package; $2\frac{1}{2} \div 18\frac{3}{4}$

Ⓒ 7 packages; $18\frac{3}{4} \div 2\frac{1}{2}$

Ⓓ 8 packages; $18\frac{3}{4} \div 2\frac{1}{2}$

PART B

Suppose that $1\frac{1}{4}$ feet of ribbon is needed to decorate a smaller package. How many more smaller packages could Franco decorate than large packages?

Name: _____

1-7 Additional Practice

In 1–3, use the table at the right.

1. Steven buys 2.32 pounds of trail mix and twice as many pounds of dried fruit. What is the total cost?

Snack Prices

Snack	Price
Dried Fruit	$4.25 per pound
Mixed Nuts	$6.75 per pound
Trail Mix	$3.50 per pound

2. Yolanda wanted to buy a total of 6 pounds of mixed nuts and dried fruit for a party. She paid $21.60 for mixed nuts and $11.90 for dried fruit. Did Yolanda buy enough mixed nuts and dried fruit for the party?

   a. What do you do first to solve the problem?

   b. What do you do next?

   c. How do you solve the problem?

3. Mario received $0.40 in change from $20.00 when he bought trail mix. How many pounds of trail mix did Mario buy?

   a. What do you do first to solve the problem?

   b. How do you solve the problem?

4. **Critique Reasoning** Students in a cooking class made $4\frac{1}{2}$ quarts of soup. They served $\frac{4}{5}$ of the soup to friends. Each serving is $\frac{3}{5}$ quart. Hector incorrectly says that there were $3\frac{3}{5}$ servings of soup. What is the correct number of servings? What did Hector do wrong?

5. **Higher Order Thinking** A hairdresser combined three bottles of shampoo into one bottle. The first bottle had 4.8 ounces of shampoo, the second bottle had 5.4 ounces, and the third bottle had 6.6 ounces. The hairdresser used $\frac{2}{5}$ of the shampoo from the new bottle when she washed her hair. How many ounces of shampoo did she use? Describe two different ways to solve the problem.

In 6 and 7, use the diagram.

The art room at a school is made up of three sections: a pottery section, a painting section, and a sculpture section.

6. Artwork will be on display for an art show in all sections of the art room except the sculpture section. How much space is available for the art show?

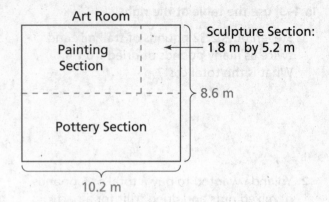

7. What is the area of the painting section?

8. Students are on a 248.5-kilometer bike trip. They rode 52.4 kilometers on the first day. They rode 0.4 of the remaining distance on the second day. How many kilometers do they have left to ride?

9. **Make Sense and Persevere** Kim made $1\frac{1}{4}$ quarts of a fruit smoothie. She drank $\frac{1}{5}$ of the smoothie. Her brothers drank the rest of the smoothie. They each had $\frac{1}{3}$ quart. How many brothers does Kim have?

10. A garden is $6\frac{2}{3}$ feet long and $2\frac{2}{3}$ feet wide. Juan is putting a brick border around the garden. Each brick is $\frac{2}{3}$ foot long. How many bricks does Juan need?

11. Margot has $21\frac{1}{2}$ pounds of flour, 8 pounds of butter, and $18\frac{1}{2}$ pounds of sugar to make shortbread cookies. If she makes 12 batches of cookies and uses all the ingredients, how many pounds of ingredients are used in each batch?

✅ Assessment Practice

12. A baker uses $13\frac{1}{2}$ cups of flour to make key lime bread. She uses $2\frac{1}{4}$ cups of flour to make each loaf. The baker sells $\frac{2}{3}$ of the loaves of bread that she makes. Which expression shows how many loaves of key lime bread the baker sells?

   Ⓐ 45 loaves; $\left(13\frac{1}{2} \div \frac{2}{3}\right) \times 2\frac{1}{4}$

   Ⓑ 20 loaves; $\left(13\frac{1}{2} \times 2\frac{1}{4}\right) \times \frac{2}{3}$

   Ⓒ 9 loaves; $\left(13\frac{1}{2} \div 2\frac{1}{4}\right) \div \frac{2}{3}$

   Ⓓ 4 loaves; $\left(13\frac{1}{2} \div 2\frac{1}{4}\right) \times \frac{2}{3}$

13. Roger ran 13.2 miles in 1.6 hours. Ana ran 10.85 miles in 1.4 hours. In miles per hour, how much faster was Roger's average speed than Ana's?

Name: _____

2-1 Additional Practice

In **1–6**, plot each point on the number line below.

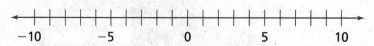

1. $L(-8)$ **2.** $M(3)$ **3.** $N(-4)$

4. $O(2)$ **5.** $P(-1)$ **6.** $Q(-6)$

In **7–12**, use the number line below. Write the integer value that each point represents, then write its opposite.

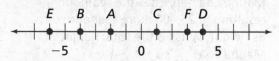

7. A **8.** B **9.** C

10. D **11.** E **12.** F

In **13–18**, write the opposite of each integer.

13. -12 **14.** 63 **15.** $-(-10)$

16. 33 **17.** -101 **18.** $-(-54)$

In **19–24**, compare the integers and write the integer with the greater value.

19. $-2, 3$ **20.** $-4, -1$ **21.** $0, -7$

22. $-(-5), 4$ **23.** $-8, -(-6)$ **24.** $-(-3), -(-1)$

25. A contestant in a game show has 9,000 points. The contestant answers the next question incorrectly and loses 750 points. What integer represents a loss of 750 points?

26. Two people are scuba diving. One diver is 36 feet below the surface. The other diver is 44 feet below the surface. What integers represent where the divers are with respect to the surface? Which diver is deeper?

Mauna Loa, in Hawaii, is the largest above-sea-level volcano.
In **27** and **28**, use the diagram of Mauna Loa.

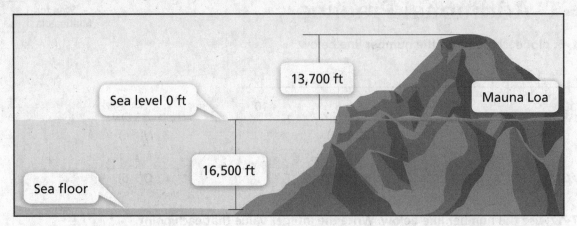

27. Reasoning Use a negative integer to represent the depth, in feet, of the sea floor.

28. Mauna Loa depresses the sea floor, resulting in 26,400 more feet added to its height. What is the total height of Mauna Loa?

29. Higher Order Thinking In math, a letter such as *p* can be assigned as a variable to represent an unknown value. Give an example of a value for *p* that results in −*p* being a positive integer. Explain.

30. Roberto and Jeanne played a difficult computer game. Roberto's final score was −60 points, and Jeanne's final score was −160 points. Use <, >, or = to compare the scores, then find the player who had the higher final score.

✓ Assessment Practice

31. Kalia goes on her first helmet diving expedition. What is a possible diving depth for her dive?

Ⓐ −4 meters

Ⓑ 0 meters

Ⓒ 4 meters

Ⓓ 40 meters

32. Fill in the bubbles to match each integer with its opposite.

	44	−9	−21	12
9	Ⓐ	Ⓑ	Ⓒ	Ⓓ
−12	Ⓔ	Ⓕ	Ⓖ	Ⓗ
−44	Ⓘ	Ⓙ	Ⓚ	Ⓛ
−(−21)	Ⓜ	Ⓝ	Ⓞ	Ⓟ

Name: _____

2-2 Additional Practice

  PRACTICE TUTORIAL

Scan for
Multimedia

In 1–8, write the number positioned at each point on the number line at the right.

1. *A*

2. *B*

3. *C*

4. *D*

5. *E*

6. *F*

7. *G*

8. *H*

In 9–16, plot each point on the number line at the right.

9. $S(2.75)$

10. $T\left(\frac{1}{4}\right)$

11. $U\left(-2\frac{1}{2}\right)$

12. $V(2.25)$

13. $W\left(1\frac{3}{4}\right)$

14. $X(-0.75)$

15. $Y(-1.75)$

16. $Z\left(-\frac{3}{1}\right)$

17. Plot -8.7 on the number line below.

-9 -8

18. Draw a number line and plot $-\frac{5}{3}$.

In 19–26, use <, >, or = to compare.

19. $-12 \bigcirc -15$

20. $-\frac{1}{3} \bigcirc -1$

21. $-2 \bigcirc -2.1$

22. $\frac{1}{5} \bigcirc \frac{1}{4}$

23. $\frac{7}{10} \bigcirc -0.85$

24. $-0.66 \bigcirc -\frac{3}{4}$

25. $-4\frac{1}{2} \bigcirc -3.9$

26. $7\frac{1}{2} \bigcirc 7.75$

In 27 and 28, use the map at the right.

27. The map shows how deep archaeologists have dug at several excavation sites. Order the archaeological excavation sites from the least depth to the greatest depth.

28. Archaeologists are excavating a new Site E. On a number line, the depth of Site E is between the depths of Site A and Site B. What is a possible depth of Site E?

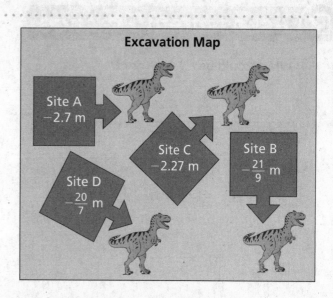

Excavation Map

Site A
-2.7 m

Site C
-2.27 m

Site B
$-\frac{21}{9}$ m

Site D
$-\frac{20}{7}$ m

Number line (right side):
3
● E
2
● B
1
● A
● H
0
● F
−1
● D
−2
● G
● C
−3

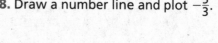

In 29–31, use the table at the right.

29. **Reasoning** Suppose you plot the lengths in the table on a number line. Which track member's long jump length would be represented by the point closest to, but not equal to, 0 on the number line? Explain.

Track Members	Long Jump Length Relative to State Qualifying Distance
Theresa	−5.625 in.
Ann	2 in.
Shirley	−3 in.
Delia	0 in.

30. Delia's relative long jump length was recorded as 0. What does this mean?

31. **Construct Arguments** Which track members did **NOT** qualify for the state championship? Construct an argument to explain how you know.

32. **Make Sense and Persevere** Order $-6\frac{1}{4}$, -6.35, $-6\frac{1}{5}$, and -6.1 from greatest to least. Explain.

33. **Higher Order Thinking** Tyler says there are infinitely many rational numbers between 0 and 1. Do you agree? Explain.

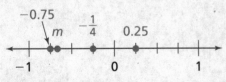
Assessment Practice

34. Which could be a value for m?

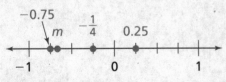

-0.75 m $-\frac{1}{4}$ 0.25

number line from -1 to 1

Ⓐ $\frac{2}{3}$

Ⓑ $\frac{1}{3}$

Ⓒ $-\frac{2}{3}$

Ⓓ $-\frac{1}{3}$

35. Which inequality represents the correct position of two numbers on a number line?

Ⓐ $6.5 > \frac{25}{4}$

Ⓑ $-6.5 > -\frac{25}{4}$

Ⓒ $-6 > -5$

Ⓓ $5 > \frac{25}{4}$

Name: _____

2-3 Additional Practice

In 1–16, find each absolute value.

1. $|-21|$

2. $|7|$

3. $\left|-\frac{3}{5}\right|$

4. $|-5.5|$

5. $\left|8\frac{3}{4}\right|$

6. $|-19.5|$

7. $\left|48\frac{3}{8}\right|$

8. $|-102.06|$

9. $|-22|$

10. $|45|$

11. $|13|$

12. $|48|$

13. $|-55.5|$

14. $\left|21\frac{1}{3}\right|$

15. $|-2.6|$

16. $|-9|$

In 17–20, order the numbers from least to greatest.

17. $|-20|, |16|, |-2|, |37|$

18. $\left|\frac{1}{4}\right|, \left|-\frac{1}{3}\right|, \left|-\frac{1}{8}\right|, |0|$

19. $|-1.5|, \left|1\frac{3}{4}\right|, |2.5|, |-2|$

20. $|6|, |0|, |-9|, |-4.2|$

21. Four submarines are exploring an undersea trench. The depth of each submarine is shown. Use absolute values to represent the distance of each submarine from sea level. Which submarine is closest to sea level?

Submarine Depths

Submarine	Depth (km)
W	−1.5
X	−3.4
Y	−2.6
Z	−4

22. Three friends started savings accounts at the same time, with the same initial deposit. The table at the right shows the total change in each friend's account after two months. List the friends in order from least to greatest total change in bank account balance.

Bank Accounts

Account Owner	Amount of Change
Louise	−$56.84
Franklin	$28.69
Hannah	$89.12

23. The table at the right shows the changes in the number of items answered correctly from a first math test to a second math test for five students. Order the students based on the least change to the greatest change.

Student	Change in Number of Correct Answers
Antoine	4
Lauren	−6
Micah	3
Beth	0
Pat	−5

24. Higher Order Thinking Is it possible that Lauren answered more questions correctly on the second math test than Antoine did? Explain.

25. Vocabulary Use <, >, or = to compare the *absolute values* of −0.3 and $\frac{1}{4}$. Explain.

26. A bird flies $13\frac{7}{10}$ feet above sea level. A fish swims $16\frac{1}{5}$ feet below sea level. Which is farther from sea level?

27. Which account's balance represents a debt greater than $50?

Account	Balance ($)
A	−60
B	−25
C	−35

☑ Assessment Practice

28. The table below shows the daily low temperatures for four days.

Day	Low Temperature
Monday	3°F
Tuesday	−4°F
Wednesday	−1°F
Thursday	2°F

PART A

Using absolute value, show the distance each temperature is from 0 degrees.

PART B

Which was the coldest day?

PRACTICE   TUTORIAL

2-4 Additional Practice

Scan for Multimedia

In 1–10, write the ordered pair for each point.

1. A   2. B

3. C   4. D

5. E   6. F

7. G   8. H

9. I   10. J

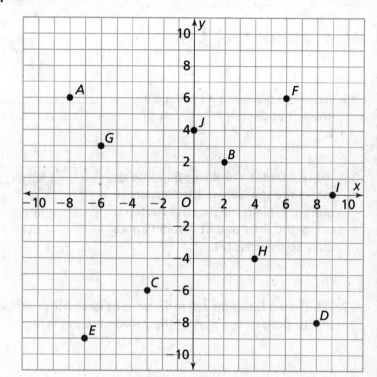

In 11–16, graph and label each point.

11. $U(-5, -3)$ 12. $V(-9, 3)$

13. $W(3, 8)$ 14. $X(8, 3)$

15. $Y(6, -6)$ 16. $Z(-5, 0)$

In 17–26, write the ordered pair for each point.

17. A   18. B

19. C   20. D

21. E   22. F

23. G   24. H

25. I   26. J

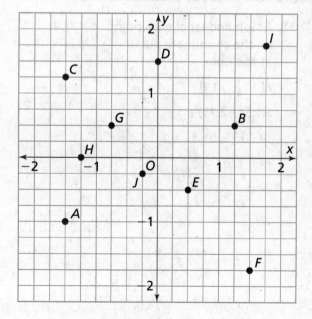

In 27–32, plot and label each point.

27. $U(1, -1.5)$ 28. $V\left(-\frac{1}{2}, 1\right)$ 29. $W\left(-1\frac{3}{4}, -1\frac{3}{4}\right)$

30. $X(1.75, -0.75)$ 31. $Y\left(0, -1\frac{3}{4}\right)$ 32. $Z\left(\frac{3}{4}, 1\right)$

In **33–37**, use the coordinate plane at the right.

33. What is located at (0.5, −0.5)?

34. What is located at $\left(-\frac{1}{2}, \frac{2}{5}\right)$?

35. Write the ordered pair to locate Brown Bat Cave.

36. Higher Order Thinking Suppose ✚ marks the spot where the treasure is buried. Explain the shortest route, using grid lines as units, from Pirate's Cove to the treasure.

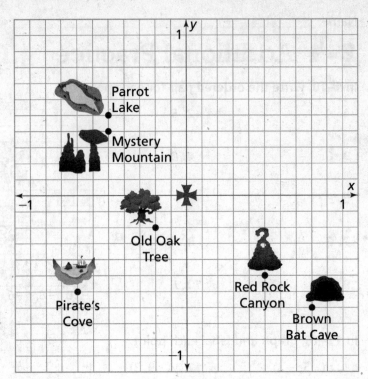

37. Which two locations are reflections of each other across one or both of the axes of the coordinate plane?

38. Graph and label each point on the coordinate plane at the right.

$E\left(-2\frac{1}{4}, -1\frac{3}{4}\right)$

$F(1.5, -2.75)$

$G(-0.75, 0)$

$H(3, 1.5)$

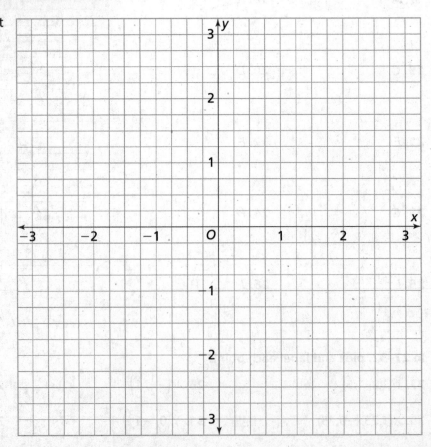

2-5 Additional Practice

Scan for Multimedia

Leveled Practice In **1–8**, find the distance between each pair of points.

1. (5, −6) and (2, −6)

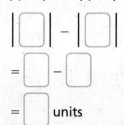

$$= \Box - \Box$$

$$= \Box \text{ units}$$

2. (−6, −4.7) and (−6, 4.1)

$$\Big| \Big| + \Big| \Big|$$

$$= \Box + \Box$$

$$= \Box \text{ units}$$

3. $\left(-2\frac{1}{2}, 1\frac{3}{4}\right)$ and $\left(-1\frac{1}{4}, 1\frac{3}{4}\right)$

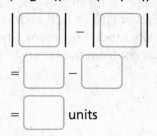

$$= \Box - \Box$$

$$= \Box \text{ units}$$

4. (−7, −4) and (−7, 9)

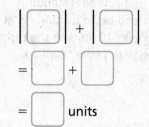

$$= \Box + \Box$$

$$= \Box \text{ units}$$

5. (2.4, 1.8) and (−0.6, 1.8)

6. $\left(7\frac{1}{2}, -6\right)$ and $\left(7\frac{1}{2}, -2\frac{1}{2}\right)$

7. (0, −6) and (−10, −6)

8. (−3, 8.5) and (−3, 7.7)

In **9–12**, use the map at the right.

9. Find the distance from the fishing area to the canoes.

10. What is the distance from the swimming area to the water slide?

11. Find the total distance from the waterfalls to the canoes and then to the fishing area.

12. Higher Order Thinking What are the coordinates of the reflection of the water slide across both axes?

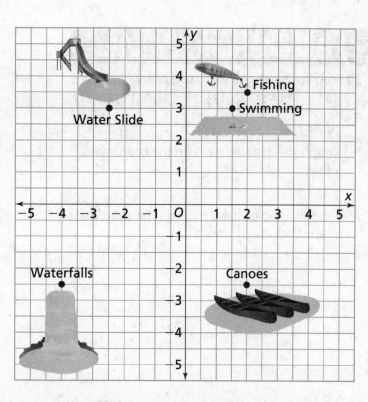

In 13–15, use the coordinate plane at the right.

The graph shows the locations of point *U* and point *V*. Point *W* is graphed at (*n*, 1). The distance from point *V* to point *W* is equal to the distance from point *V* to point *U*.

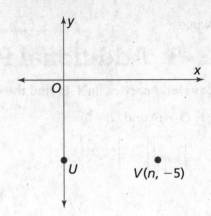

13. What is the distance from point *V* to point *W*?

14. What is the value of *n*?

15. What are the coordinates of point *U*, point *V*, and point *W*?

16. **Reasoning** On a map, Jorge is standing at (11, −11). His friend Leslie is standing at (1, −11). If Jorge walks 10 units to the right, will he be standing with Leslie? Explain.

17. On a map, a museum is located at (15, −2). A library is located at (15, −17). If each unit on the map is a city block, how many city blocks is the museum from the library?

18. Write four examples of ordered pairs, each located in a different quadrant of the coordinate plane.

19. Airport A is located on a coordinate plane at (−18, 14). Airport B is located at (8, 14). How far apart are the airports?

✅ Assessment Practice

20. You are given the following ordered pairs.

$$\left(4\tfrac{1}{2}, -1\right) \left(-1\tfrac{1}{4}, 2\tfrac{1}{2}\right) \left(2\tfrac{1}{4}, 2\tfrac{1}{2}\right) \left(5\tfrac{1}{2}, 1\tfrac{1}{2}\right) \left(5\tfrac{1}{2}, -2\tfrac{1}{2}\right)$$

PART A

Graph the ordered pairs on the coordinate plane.

PART B

Find the two ordered pairs on the coordinate plane that are $3\tfrac{1}{2}$ units apart.

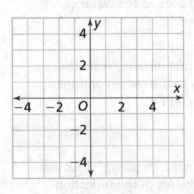

PRACTICE   TUTORIAL

2-6 Additional Practice

Scan for
Multimedia

In 1 and 2, use the coordinate plane at the right.

1. What is the perimeter of rectangle *ABCD*?

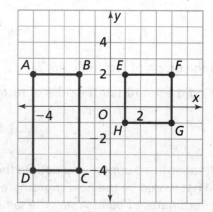

2. What is the perimeter of square *EFGH*?

3. Polygon *QRST* has vertices $Q\left(4\frac{1}{2}, 2\right)$, $R\left(8\frac{1}{2}, 2\right)$, $S\left(8\frac{1}{2}, -3\frac{1}{2}\right)$, and $T\left(4\frac{1}{2}, -3\frac{1}{2}\right)$. Is polygon *QRST* a rectangle? Justify your answer.

4. You draw a rectangle with vertices at $(-3.5, 3)$, $(3.5, 3)$, $(3.5, -3)$, and $(-3.5, -3)$. What is the perimeter and area of the rectangle?

In 5–7, use the coordinate plane at the right.

5. Madison used a coordinate plane to map out an L-shaped herb garden, shown at the right. Each unit on the grid represents $\frac{1}{2}$ yard. To buy a fence for the garden, she needs to know its perimeter. What is the perimeter of the garden?

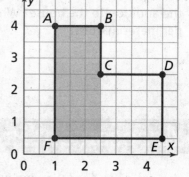

6. Madison plants rosemary in the shaded section of the garden. What is the perimeter of the shaded section?

7. Madison plants sage in the unshaded section of the garden. What is the perimeter of the unshaded section?

8. Higher Order Thinking A rectangle on a coordinate plane has one vertex at $(-5, -6)$ and a perimeter of 30 units. What could be the coordinates of the other 3 vertices?

9. Use Structure Mr. Wells drew a plan for a rectangular dog run. The vertices are $\left(2\frac{1}{3}, 7\frac{1}{2}\right)$, $\left(12, 7\frac{1}{2}\right)$, $(12, 1)$, and $\left(2\frac{1}{3}, 1\right)$. What is the perimeter of the dog run?

10. Use the graph of rectangle *ABCD*.

a. Find the lengths of the sides of rectangle *ABCD*.

b. **Reasoning** Suppose you double the length of each side. What would be the new coordinates of point *C* if the coordinates of point *A* stay the same? Explain.

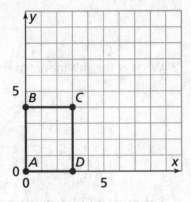

11. Sheila is building an addition to a house. The points $E\left(-1\frac{1}{2}, -2\frac{1}{2}\right)$, $F\left(4\frac{1}{2}, -2\frac{1}{2}\right)$, $G\left(4\frac{1}{2}, 3\frac{1}{2}\right)$, and $H\left(-1\frac{1}{2}, 3\frac{1}{2}\right)$ are the points she plotted on a coordinate plane to draw the new room plan. What is the shape of the addition to the house? What is the perimeter in units?

12. On a math test, the students are asked to find the perimeter of rectangle *STUV* with vertices $S(-6.5, -8.5)$, $T(2.5, -8.5)$, $U(2.5, 3.5)$, and $V(-6.5, 3.5)$. Alberto writes that the perimeter of the rectangle is 18 units. Is he correct? Explain.

✓ Assessment Practice

13. You are given the following points on a coordinate plane: $X(-3, 3.3)$, $Y(-3, -5.2)$, and $Z(4.5, -5.2)$.

PART A

Using absolute value, find the distance (number of units) between points *X* and *Y*.

PART B

Select all the coordinates that are 5 units from point *Z*.

☐ $(-0.5, -10.2)$

☐ $(4.5, -0.2)$

☐ $(-0.5, -5.2)$

☐ $(9.5, -0.2)$

☐ $(4.5, -5.2)$

Name: _____

3-1 Additional Practice

In 1–3, write the base number for each expression.

1. 5^{12}

2. 1.2^2

3. $\left(\frac{1}{3}\right)^4$

In 4–6, write the exponent for each expression.

4. $7 \times 7 \times 7 \times 7$

5. $\left(\frac{2}{3}\right)^8$

6. $0.5 \times 0.5 \times 0.5$

In 7–8, write each power as repeated multiplication. Then evaluate.

7. 3^4

8. $\left(\frac{1}{7}\right)^2$

In 9–12, evaluate each expression.

9. 9^3

10. $\left(\frac{1}{4}\right)^3$

11. 99^0

12. 1.5×10^4

13. Is the sum of the areas of two smaller squares equal to the area of a large square if the side lengths of the squares are 8 feet, 5 feet, and 3 feet? Note that the area of a square is s^2, where s is the side length. Explain.

14. Lexi bought a new car. She drove 5^4 miles in the first month that she owned the car and 4^5 miles in the second month that she owned the car. How many miles did Lexi drive in all during the first two months that she owned the car?

15. **Construct Arguments** Is 0.3^4 equal to 0.9^2? Explain.

16. What are two ways that you can represent 27 using 3?

17. Dustin computed his family's road trip as 4.43×10^3 miles. How many miles did Dustin's family travel on the road trip?

18. The area of the Great Lakes is about 9.5×10^4 square miles. About how many square miles is the area of the Great Lakes?

19. Reasoning What is the value of 1^{102}? What is the value of any power of 1? Justify your answer.

20. Humans can distinguish up to 18,400,000 individual dots called pixels on a typical computer display. Can a human distinguish pixels on a same-sized HDTV with 2×10^6 pixels? Explain.

21. Higher Order Thinking In case of an emergency, the school has a calling list so that everyone is called in the least amount of time. Each of the first 3 people on the list calls another 3 people on the list. Then, each of the people in the second group calls another 3 people on the list, and so on. The fifth group of people will make 243 calls. Is this statement accurate? Explain.

22. Use Structure An investment of $1 was put in an account. Every 8 years, the money doubled. No additional money was added to the account. Would the expression $1 \times 2 \times 2 \times 2 \times 2 \times 2 \times 2$ correctly represent how much was in the investment account after 48 years? Explain.

☑ Assessment Practice

23. Select all expressions equivalent to $0.5 \cdot 0.5 \cdot 0.5$.

☐ $0.5^2 \times 0.5^2$

☐ 0.5^3

☐ $5^2 \times 5^1$

☐ $3^{0.5}$

☐ 0.5×3

24. Which expression is equivalent to 343?

Ⓐ 8^3

Ⓑ $6 \times 6 \times 6$

Ⓒ 7^3

Ⓓ $7 \times 7 \times 7 \times 7$

Name: _____

3-2 Additional Practice

In 1–4, find the prime factorization of each number. If it is prime, write *prime*.

1. 90   2. 66   3. 52   4. 41

In 5–8, find the GCF for each pair of numbers.

5. 45, 60   6. 24, 100   7. 19, 22   8. 14, 28

In 9–12, use the GCF and the Distributive Property to find each sum.

9. 32 + 48   10. 15 + 57

11. 98 + 14   12. 55 + 88

In 13–16, find the LCM of each pair of numbers.

13. 8, 12   14. 6, 7   15. 3, 4   16. 4, 9

17. **Reasoning** Mrs. James displayed the factor tree at the right. Complete the factor tree to find the number that has a prime factorization of $2^4 \times 3$.

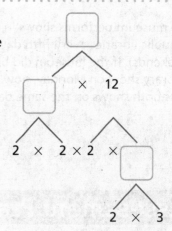

18. **Higher Order Thinking** The student council was preparing for the school bake sale. The members divided each type of donated item equally on plates. Each plate contained only one type of item, and every plate had exactly the same number of items. There were no leftovers. What is the greatest number of items that could have been placed on each plate?

Bake Sale Donations	
Muffins	96
Breadsticks	48
Rolls	84

19. Critique Reasoning Ron is trying to find the LCM of 4 and 6. His work is shown at the right. What is Ron's mistake? Explain how to find the correct LCM of 4 and 6.

4: (2 x 2)

6: (2 x 3)

2 x 2 x 2 x 3 = 24, so the LCM of 4 and 6 is 24.

---

20. Peanuts are sold in 8-ounce and 12-ounce packages. What is the fewest number of ounces you can buy of each package to have equal amounts of each package size?

21. Al's garden is 18 feet long and 30 feet wide. He wants to put fence posts the same distance apart along all sides of the garden. What is the greatest distance apart that Al can place the fence posts?

In 22 and 23, use the diagram at the right.

22. At what times between 10:00 A.M. and 5:00 P.M. do the chemistry presentation and the recycling presentation start simultaneously?

Science Museum
— Show Schedule —
Chemistry — Every 10 minutes
Electricity — Every 20 minutes
Recycling — Every 6 minutes
Fossils — Every 45 minutes
The first showing for all shows is at 10:00 A.M.

23. The museum performs shows in schools every Monday and in public libraries every fifth day (on both weekdays and weekends). If the museum did both a school show and a library show on Monday, how many days will it be until it does both shows on the same day again?

✓ Assessment Practice

24. Match each pair of numbers with the pair of numbers that has the same LCM.

	Same LCM as 6, 8	Same LCM as 4, 10	Same LCM as 5, 8	Same LCM as 8, 20
8, 10	☐	☐	☐	☐
4, 5	☐	☐	☐	☐

25. Which expression is equivalent to 42 + 70?

Ⓐ 6(7 + 10)

Ⓑ 7(7 + 10)

Ⓒ 14(3 + 5)

Ⓓ 21(2 + 3)

3-3 Additional Practice

Leveled Practice In **1–3**, use the order of operations to evaluate.

1. $0.2^2 \div [7.9 - (4.1 + 1.8)]$

$= 0.2^2 \div [7.9 - \boxed{}]$

$= 0.2^2 \div \boxed{}$

$= \boxed{} \div \boxed{}$

$= \boxed{}$

2. $(14.7 + 9.3) \times \left(\frac{1}{2}\right)^2$

$= \boxed{} \times \left(\frac{1}{2}\right)^2$

$= \boxed{} \times \boxed{}$

$= \boxed{}$

3. $12.3 + (6^2 - 11.8) - 1$

$= 12.3 + (\boxed{} - 11.8) - 1$

$= 12.3 + \boxed{} - 1$

$= \boxed{} - 1$

$= \boxed{}$

In **4–6**, evaluate each expression.

4. $5^2 - 9 \div 3$

5. $8 + 6 - 2 \times 2 - 3^2$

6. $4^2 \div [(3.2 \times 2) + 1.6]$

In **7–9**, insert grouping symbols so that the expression has the given value.

7. Target value: 29

$12 \times 2^2 - 18.4 + 0.6$

8. Target value: 23

$5^2 - 0.2 \times 8 + 12 \times \frac{1}{2}$

9. Target value: 45

$19 + 1^5 \div \frac{1}{2} + 5$

10. Nikki's backyard is in the shape of a rectangle. The length is 27 feet. The width is one-third the length plus 4 feet. Write and evaluate an expression to find the area of Nikki's backyard.

11. Make Sense and Persevere Write a numerical expression, with at least three operations, that has the same value as $(12 - 9)^2 \times (4 + 3)$. Justify your answer.

12. Critique Reasoning Ivy's basketball team scored 38 points in the first game of the season. In the next two games they scored a total of 77 points. For every point scored, $0.50 is put in a jar to use for a party after the season. Ivy says that you can use the expression $38 + 77 \times 0.5$ to find how much money is in the jar after the third game. Is she correct? Explain.

13. A printing error in a math book removed the brackets and parentheses from a numerical expression. Rewrite the expression $3^2 + 7 \times 4 + 5$ with parentheses so that it is equivalent to 69.

14. Jessica bought a new computer for $800. She put $120 down and got a student discount of $50. Her mother gave her $\frac{1}{2}$ of the balance for her birthday. Use the numerical expression to find the amount that Jessica still owes for the computer.

$[800 - (120 + 50)] \div 2$

15. Luke needs a new fence around his garden, but the gate across the narrow end of the garden will not be replaced. Write and evaluate a numerical expression to find how many feet of fencing Luke needs.

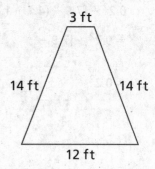

3 ft

14 ft   14 ft

12 ft

16. Hailey walks at an average rate of 3.5 miles per hour. Last month, she walked 3 weeks at her regular rate for 6 hours per week. She walked 1 week at one-half her regular rate for 4 hours. Write and evaluate a numerical expression to find the total number of miles Hailey walked last month.

17. Higher Order Thinking James says that he used grouping symbols to find four equal values for $2^3 + 3 \times 9 - 4^2$. He wrote these expressions:

$2^3 + 3 \times 9 - 4^2$

$(2^3 + 3) \times 9 - 4^2$

$2^3 + 3 \times (9 - 4)^2$

$2^3 + (3 \times 9 - 4^2)$

Do you agree with James? Explain.

18. Select all expressions equivalent to $102.4 - [(2^3 \times 3) + 13.8] \div 7$.

☐ $102.4 - [(3^2 \times 3) + 13.8] \div 7$

☐ $(10^2 + 2.4) - (37.8 \div 7)$

☐ $102.4 - (6^2 + 1.8) \div 7$

☐ $102.4 - [(2^3 \times 3) + 20.8]$

☐ $(60 + 42.4) - [(8 \times 3) + 13.8] \times 7$

19. Which value is equivalent to the expression $[(7.3 + 3.6) - 4.7] + 1.8 - 2^2$?

ⓐ 4

ⓑ 0.4

ⓒ 40

ⓓ −4

3-4 Additional Practice

Scan for
Multimedia

In 1–10, write an algebraic expression for each situation.

1. 6 more than a number c

2. 2.5 less than a number d

3. 50 divided by a number f

4. twice a number n

5. 12 fewer than h hats

6. 4 times the sum of x and $\frac{1}{2}$

7. 6 less than the quotient of z divided by 3

8. twice a number k plus the quantity s minus 2

9. 8 more than s stripes

10. 5 times the quantity m divided by 2

In 11–14, tell how many terms each expression has.

11. $4c + 7\frac{1}{2}$

12. $80.6 - 3p - q$

13. $(7 \cdot 2) \div s$

14. $100 + (8 \cdot 6) - 50 + 2$

In 15 and 16, use the expression $1 + \frac{z}{3} + 2w$.

15. Which part of the expression is a quotient? Describe its parts.

16. Which part of the expression is a product of two factors? Describe its parts.

In 17–20, use the sign at the right.

17. A pet store is having a pet fish sale. Lenny bought p platies and l loaches. Write an algebraic expression to represent the total cost of the fish.

18. **Model with Math** Mr. Bolden bought g guppies and paid with a $20 bill. Write an algebraic expression to represent how much change Mr. Bolden got back.

Pet Fish Sale

Guppy	$3
Loach	$4
Platy	$2
Tetra	$5

19. **Make Sense and Persevere** Ms. Wilson bought two bags of pet fish for her twin nieces. Each bag has g guppies and one tetra. Ms. Wilson also bought one box of fish food that cost d dollars. Write an algebraic expression to represent how much she paid in all.

20. In 3 days, the pet store sold 27 guppies. In the same time, the store sold twice as many platies as guppies. Evaluate the expression below to find the dollar amount of sales of guppies and platies.

$27 \cdot 3 + (2 \cdot 27) \cdot 2$

21. **Higher Order Thinking** Describe a situation that can be represented by the algebraic expression $6b + w$.

22. **Critique Reasoning** Mary says that the expression $\frac{a}{2}$ has no terms because there are no plus or minus signs. Explain whether her reasoning is correct.

☑ Assessment Practice

23. Which algebraic expression represents the following situation: *Six fewer seashells than the total number of seashells in p packages, each of which has five seashells?*

   Ⓐ $6p + 5$

   Ⓑ $5p + 6$

   Ⓒ $5p - 6$

   Ⓓ $6p - 5$

24. Select all of the phrases that could be represented by the algebraic expression $3n - 3$.

   ☐ three fewer than a number n

   ☐ the difference between a number n and three

   ☐ three fewer than three times a number n

   ☐ the product of three and a number n

   ☐ three less than the product of three and a number n

3-5 Additional Practice

Scan for Multimedia

In 1–8, find the value of each expression when
$a = \frac{1}{3}$, $b = 9$, $c = 5$, and $d = 10$.

1. $6a + 4$

2. $5a - \frac{2}{3}$

3. $5d \div c + 2$

4. $b^2 - 9a$

5. $12a + c - b$

6. $\frac{1}{2}d + c^2 - b$

7. $d^2 \div 2c - b + 3a$

8. $3c + b^2 \div 27a - d$

In 9–11, evaluate each expression for $x = 3.1$, $x = 6.2$, and $x = 8.3$.

9. $5x$

10. $8.2 + x \div 2$

11. $2x + 1.5x$

In 12 and 13, evaluate each expression for the set of values given in the table.

12.

c	1	2	3
$28 - c^3 + 6$			

13.

t	0.01	1	2.5
$\frac{9.5}{t} + 3.2t$			

In 14 and 15, use the table at the right.

14. Model with Math Tamera has a pet-sitting business. The table shows how much she charges. Last week, she sat for one dog and for two cats.

Number of Pets	Per Day	Per Hour
One dog	$20	$7
Two dogs	$25	$9
One or two cats	$15	$6

   a. Suppose that Tamera spent h hours sitting the dog and 2 days sitting the cats. Write an expression that shows how much she earned.

   b. Evaluate the expression you wrote to find how much Tamera earned if she sat 2 hours for the dog.

15. For any of the pet-sitting services listed in the table, how many hours can you purchase before it would be cheaper to pay for one day?

16. **Higher Order Thinking** The deli sells ham for $3.95 per pound, turkey for $4.30 per pound, and cheese for $3.10 per pound. Write an expression that shows how much it will cost to buy h pounds of ham, t pounds of turkey, and c pounds of cheese. Then find the cost for 1 pound of ham, 1.5 pounds of turkey, and 2.3 pounds of cheese.

17. **Model with Math** Juan rented a paddleboard for $5.75 per hour plus a $17.50 fee. Write an expression that shows how much it will cost Juan to rent the paddleboard for x hours. Then evaluate the expression for 3 hours.

18. **Be Precise** The table shows how much a frozen yogurt shop charges for its yogurt. Write an expression to show how much it costs to buy a small yogurt with no toppings and a large yogurt with x toppings. Then find the total cost for a small yogurt with no toppings and a large yogurt with 3 toppings.

Size of Cup	Cost of Cup	Cost per Topping
Small	$2.85	$0.25
Medium	$3.75	$0.30
Large	$4.65	$0.35

19. A school district can send a representative to the state spelling bee for every 50 students in the school district that year. There are 5 schools with a, b, c, d, and e students, respectively.

   a. Write an algebraic expression to show how many representatives, r, the school district will have in any year.

   b. The table shows the number of students at each school this year. Use your expression to find the number of students the school district can send to the state spelling bee this year. Does your answer make sense? Explain.

District Schools This Year
1,587 students
985 students
2,052 students
824 students
752 students

☑ Assessment Practice

20. An equation is shown.

   $3r - (r + 0.47) = 3.13$

   Which value of r makes the equation true?

   Ⓐ 0.8

   Ⓑ 1.7

   Ⓒ 1.8

   Ⓓ 2.8

3-6 Additional Practice

Leveled Practice In **1–10**, write equivalent expressions.

1. $5(m - 2) = \boxed{}\, m - \boxed{}$

2. $2\left(9p - \frac{1}{2}\right) = \boxed{}\, p - \boxed{}$

3. $6(8x + 1)$

4. $35x + 30$

5. $6\left(3y - \frac{1}{2}\right)$

6. $1.6 + (2z + 0.4)$

7. $8w - 16$

8. $2.2x + 2.2$

9. $100(z^2 - 5.38)$

10. $8 \cdot \left(y^3 \cdot \frac{3}{4}\right)$

In **11–14**, write the letter(s) of the expressions that are equivalent to the given expression.

11. $5x + 5$

   a. $10x + 5 - 5x$

   b. $10x$

   c. $5(x + 1)$

12. $12x - 10 - 6x$

   a. $6x - 10$

   b. $2(3x - 5)$

   c. $16x - 8 - 2$

13. $\frac{1}{2}x + 3 + \frac{1}{2}x$

   a. $\frac{1}{2}(x + 3)$

   b. $x + 3$

   c. $3x + 3 - x$

14. $3(3x - 1)$

   a. $6x - 2$

   b. $9x - 3$

   c. $15x + 6 - 6x - 3$

In **15** and **16**, use the sign at the right.

15. Model with Math Ms. Thomas ordered 5 pencil packs, n notebooks, and 5 sets of markers. Write an algebraic expression that represents the cost of Ms. Thomas's order.

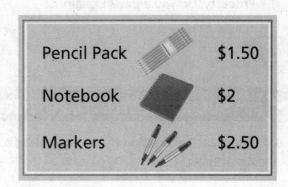

Pencil Pack	$1.50
Notebook	$2
Markers	$2.50

16. Use Structure Use properties of operations to write an expression equivalent to the expression you wrote in Exercise 15.

In 17–19, use the sign at the right.

17. Write an algebraic expression that represents each purchase.

   a. Ms. Martinez bought x number of litter boxes and 8 bags of cat food for the animal shelter.

   b. Two sisters each bought 1 litter box, 10 cat toys, and x bags of cat food.

Cat Toy	$4
Cat Food	$12
Litter Box	$16

18. **Make Sense and Persevere** Suppose that x has the same value in both of the expressions you wrote in Exercise 17. Are the two expressions you wrote equivalent? Explain.

19. **Construct Arguments** Which costs the most: 12 cat toys, 4 bags of cat food, or 3 litter boxes? Explain.

20. **Model with Math** The formula for the perimeter of a rectangle is $2\ell + 2w$, where ℓ is the length and w is the width. How can you use the Distributive Property to write an equivalent expression for $2\ell + 2w$?

21. **Higher Order Thinking** Explain why the expression you wrote in Exercise 20 may be easier to use than $2\ell + 2w$.

22. **Critique Reasoning** Zach says that the expressions $6x - 36$ and $3(2x - 12)$ are equivalent because of the Distributive Property. Do you agree? Explain.

23. Are the two expressions shown below equivalent? Explain.

   $4n + 6m - 12k$ and $2(2n + 3m - 6k)$

☑ Assessment Practice

24. Select each expression that is equivalent to $4\frac{1}{2} + \left(3t + 1\frac{1}{2}\right)$.

   ☐ $\left(4\frac{1}{2} + 3t\right) + 1\frac{1}{2}$

   ☐ $\left(4\frac{1}{2} + 1\frac{1}{2}\right) + 3t$

   ☐ $3(2 + t)$

   ☐ $3 + 6$

   ☐ $9t$

25. Select each expression that is equivalent to $8x - 24$.

   ☐ $8(x - 3)$

   ☐ $8(x - 24)$

   ☐ $9(x - 3) - (x - 3)$

   ☐ $(5 + 3)x - 24$

   ☐ $16x$

3-7 Additional Practice

Leveled Practice In **1–13**, combine like terms to simplify each expression.

1. $1\frac{1}{2}z^2 + 3\frac{1}{2} + 5z - 3 + 6z - \frac{1}{2}z^2$

$= (\boxed{}z^2 - \boxed{}z^2) + (\boxed{}z + \boxed{}z) + (\boxed{} - \boxed{})$

$= \boxed{}z^2 + \boxed{}z + \boxed{}$

2. $4y + 9y$

3. $3z + \frac{3}{4} - 2z$

4. $25 + 5w - 10 + w$

5. $7.7w - 4.6w$

6. $\frac{1}{2}x + \frac{1}{2} + \frac{1}{2}x + \frac{1}{2}$

7. $12y^2 - 6y^2$

8. $3z^3 + 2\frac{1}{4} - z^3$

9. $6.6m + 3m$

10. $100n - 1 - 25n$

11. $5x + \frac{1}{2} + 3y + \frac{1}{4} + 2x - 2y$

12. $p^2 + 2.3 + 3p^2$

13. $z^4 + z^4 + z^4 + z^4$

14. Model with Math Shea sells bracelets at the farmer's market. For each bracelet she sells, she spends $1.50 on beads and $3.00 on hardware. She also pays $10 per day to rent a booth.

a. Write an expression that represents Shea's total expenses for selling x bracelets per day in 4 days.

b. How can you use a property of operations to write a simplified equivalent expression?

15. Jose is training for a half-marathon. Each week he runs x miles per day for 5 days. For 3 days of the week, he runs at a speed of 8 minutes per mile. For 2 days he runs 7-minute miles.

a. Write an expression to represent the amount of time, in minutes, that Jose runs in 4 weeks.

b. Write an expression that is equivalent to the expression you wrote above. Explain how you know the expressions are equivalent.

In 16–18, use the sign at the right.

16. **Model with Math** At a drive-through restaurant, Casey's family ordered a small drink and m medium drinks. Anika's family ordered m medium drinks and a large drink. Write an algebraic expression that shows the total cost, in dollars, of both orders.

Small $1.10

Medium $1.25

Large $1.50

17. **Use Structure** Combine like terms to write an expression that is equivalent to the expression you wrote in Exercise 16.

18. Show that the two expressions are equivalent.

19. Jan rewrote the expression $\frac{1}{2}y \cdot 5$ as $5 \cdot \frac{1}{2}y$. Which property of operations did Jan use?

20. **Construct Arguments** Emma wrote $8.4x + 6.3x + 12.6$ as an equivalent expression for $4.2(2x + 1.5x + 3)$. She said that her equivalent expression is simplified. Do you agree? Explain.

21. **Critique Reasoning** Manuel rewrote the expression $6x - x + 5$ as $6 + 5$. Are $6x - x + 5$ and $6 + 5$ equivalent expressions? Explain.

22. **Higher Order Thinking** Write an equivalent expression for the expression shown below. Explain.

$$\frac{b}{2} + \frac{b}{2}$$

Assessment Practice

23. Select all expressions that are equivalent to $8\frac{1}{2}x + \frac{1}{2} + 3\frac{1}{2}x - 2x$.

   ☐ $12x - 2x$

   ☐ $10x + \frac{1}{2}$

   ☐ $12 - 2x$

   ☐ $9x + 3\frac{1}{2} - 2x$

   ☐ $12x - 2x + \frac{1}{2}$

24. Which is an equivalent expression to $\frac{1}{2}x + 4\frac{1}{2} + \frac{1}{2}x - \frac{1}{2}$?

   Ⓐ $\frac{1}{2}x + 4\frac{1}{2}$

   Ⓑ $x + 5$

   Ⓒ $x + 4$

   Ⓓ $\frac{1}{2}x - 4\frac{1}{2}$

4-1 Additional Practice

In 1–10, tell which given value, if any, is the solution of the equation.

1. $5.6 = l + 4.09$ $l = 0.7, 0.97, 1.51, 9.69$

2. $5k = 65$ $k = 11, 12, 13, 14$

3. $t - \$5.60 = \$1.04$ $t = \$6.00, \$6.10, \$6.64, \$7.00$

4. $133 \div y = 19$ $y = 6, 7, 8, 9$

5. $14 = \dfrac{u}{6}$ $u = 78, 81, 84, 90$

6. $9 + a = 46$ $a = 37, 39, 41, 55$

7. $6.8 = 2.89 + m$ $m = 3.9, 3.91, 4, 4.11$

8. $8c = 64$ $c = 6, 7, 8, 9$

9. $d \div 5.20 = 2.40$ $d = 10.92, 16.12, 17.68$

10. $m - 63.28 = 14.92$ $m = 77.86, 78.15, 79.20$

11. Anton walked 8.9 miles of his 13.5-mile goal for this week. Use the equation $m + 8.9 = 13.5$ to find which path Anton should walk so that he meets his goal for the week.

Path Lengths	
Meadow Path	3.2 miles
Circle Path	4.2 miles
Oak Tree Path	4.6 miles

12. Brandon has 132 petunia plants and 6 planters. He and his helpers will put x plants in each planter and have none left over. Which of Brandon's three helpers, if any, correctly guessed how many plants are to be planted in each planter? Use the equation $6x = 132$.

Helper	Guess
Troy	20 plants
Bethany	25 plants
Lacy	30 plants

13. **Higher Order Thinking** James bought a movie ticket and popcorn for $12.20. The movie ticket cost $8.45. Use the equation $c + \$8.45 = \$12.20$ to find which size popcorn James bought. How much change did James get if he paid with a $20 bill?

Cost of Popcorn	
Small	$2.85
Medium	$3.75
Large	$4.75
Extra Large	$4.85

14. **Reasoning** Kyle bought a movie ticket for $8.45 and a drink for $1.80. He had just enough money remaining to buy a large popcorn. How much money did Kyle start with? Write an equation to show your reasoning.

15. Nadia made 56 muffins. She wants to fill each treat bag with 8 muffins. Nadia bought 7 bags. Use the equation $56 \div b = 8$ to explain whether Nadia bought enough bags.

16. A math exercise states that the circumference of a certain circle is 23.55 inches with diameter d and π rounded to 3.14. Larry says the diameter is 5 inches; Rosie says it is 8 inches; and Rashida says it is 6.5 inches. Which, if any, of the students is correct? Use the equation $3.14d = 23.55$ to justify your answer.

✓ Assessment Practice

17. Jerry built a table with a square top. The perimeter of the tabletop is 18 feet. He knows that the side length of the table is 3, $3\frac{1}{4}$, 4, or $4\frac{1}{2}$ feet. Use the equation $18 = 4s$, where s is the side length of the table, to determine the side length of the tabletop. Explain how you found your answer.

4-2 Additional Practice

In 1–6, tell which property of equality was used.

1. $49 = \frac{245}{v}$

    $49 \times 65 = \left(\frac{245}{v}\right) \times 65$

2. $14 + s = 28$

    $(14 + s) - 2 = 28 - 2$

3. $4y = 48$

    $4y \div 4 = 48 \div 4$

4. $88 = 33 + 5x$

    $88 - 33 = (33 + 5x) - 33$

5. $d - 33 = 34$

    $d - 33 + 33 = 34 + (30 + 3)$

6. $3m + 14 = 19$

    $3m + 14 - 14 = 19 - (19 - 5)$

In 7–12, answer yes or no and explain why or why not.

7. If $10 \times 3 = 30$, does $10 \times 3 + 4 = 30 + 5$?

8. If $8n = 180$, does $8n \div 8 = 180 \div 8$?

9. If $d \div 3 = 10$, does $d \div 3 + 3 = 10 + 3$?

10. If $12 - 2 = 10$, does $12 - 2 - 3 = 10 - 2$?

11. If $4s - 2 = 12$, does $(4s - 2) \div 2 = 12 \div 2$?

12. If $\frac{g}{5} = 8 + 9$, does $\frac{g}{5} + 9 = 8 + 9$?

13. **Critique Reasoning** In math class, you are checking how a friend balanced an equation. His work is at the right. What error did your friend make? Explain.

    > Unbalanced equation:
    >
    > $16 \div 8 = 16 \div 8 - 1$
    >
    > Balanced equation:
    >
    > $16 \div 8 + 1 = 16 \div 8 - 1$

14. James multiplies one side of the equation $56 + 124 = 180$ by a number n. What does James need to do to balance the equation?

15. Construct Arguments Maggie said that she could add 8 to both sides of any equation and the expressions on both sides of the equation would still be equal. Do you agree? Explain.

16. Reasoning If you are given a true equation and you multiply each side by the same number, the resulting equation is also a true equation. If you are given a false equation and you multiply each side by the same number, will the resulting equation be a true equation or a false equation? Give an example to explain.

17. Higher Order Thinking A store sells 3 pens in a package. There are 12 packages of pens in a box. Write an equation to model the number of pens in a box. Use the equation to write another equation that uses the Subtraction Property of Equality. Explain how the equation is balanced.

18. Corky writes four equations to show each of the properties of equality. Which of Corky's equations is incorrect? Explain.

Properties of Equality	
Addition	$3 + 4 = a$ $(3 + 4) + 2 = a + 2$
Subtraction	$3 + 4 = a$ $(3 + 4) - 2 = a - 2$
Multiplication	$3 + 4 = a$ $4(3 + 4) = 4a$
Division	$3 + 4 = a$ $\dfrac{(3 + 4)}{2} = 2 \div a$

☑ Assessment Practice

19. Which equation is equivalent to $5 = 95 \div x$?

Ⓐ $5 = (95 \div x) + 6$

Ⓑ $5 + 6 = (95 \div x) + 6$

Ⓒ $5 + 6 = (95 \div x) \times 6$

Ⓓ $5 \div 6 = (95 \div x) + 6$

20. Which equation is **NOT** equivalent to $5 + n = 10$? Select all that apply.

☐ $5 + n - n = 10 - n$

☐ $5 + n - 5 = 10 - 10$

☐ $5 + n - 5 = 10 - 5$

☐ $5 + n + 3 = 10 + 3$

☐ $5 + n - 10 = 10 - 5$

4-3 Additional Practice

In 1 and 2, write an equation and solve for the variable.

1.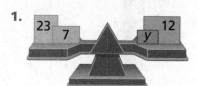

23 7 12 y

2.

3 a 15 8 8 8

In 3–8, solve each equation.

3. $g - 8 = 25$

4. $25 + y = 42$

5. $r + 82 = 97$

6. $30 = m - 18$

7. $150 = e + 42$

8. $a - 51 = 12$

9. Only 12 students can be in the next school play. Let t represent the number of students who tried out for the play. The number of students who tried out but did not get a role is 42.

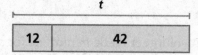

t

| 12 | 42 |

  a. Explain how the bar diagram and the equation $t - 12 = 42$ model this situation.

  b. Solve the equation to find the total number of students who tried out for the play.

10. Shree writes the equation $x + 7 = 28$. What should Shree do to find the value of x?

11. Krystal says that you need to add to solve the subtraction equation $y - 11 = 52$. Is Krystal correct? Explain.

12. Let *a* equal the measure of angle *A*. The equation $360° = a + 90° + 135° + 75°$ represents the sum of the angles in the quadrilateral. Find the missing angle measure by solving the equation.

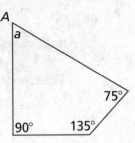

13. Higher Order Thinking In the equation $8x - 1 = 3x + 4$ the variable *x* represents the same value. Which value of *x* is the solution of the equation; *x* = 0, 1, 2, or 3? Explain.

14. This year, a rancher counted 225 horses on the range. This count is 22 fewer than last year. How many horses did the rancher count last year? Let *h* be the number of horses counted last year. Solve $h - 22 = 225$ to find the number of horses counted last year.

15. Model with Math Jorge hiked 15.4 miles on Monday. He hiked 20.6 miles on Tuesday, and the rest of the 50-mile trail on Wednesday. If *m* represents the miles Jorge hiked on Wednesday, write an equation to show the total number of miles Jorge hiked and solve for *m*.

16. A volunteer made *m* muffins for a bake sale. After selling 28 muffins, 21 muffins remained. The equation $m - 28 = 21$ represents the situation. What is the first step in writing an equivalent equation to solve $m - 28 = 21$?

17. Construct Arguments Explain how to solve for *n* in the equation $n + 25 = 233$.

✓ Assessment Practice

18. Which equation has $h = 5$ as the solution?

Ⓐ $51 - h = 46$

Ⓑ $44 + h = 51$

Ⓒ $h - 4 = 5$

Ⓓ $7h = 42$

19. Select all the equations that have the same solution as $44 = x + 39$.

☐ $33 = 27 + x$

☐ $x + 11 = 16$

☐ $4 = x - 4$

☐ $24 = x + 19$

☐ $26 = x + 21$

4-4 Additional Practice

Scan for
Multimedia

In **1–4**, explain how to isolate the variable in each equation.

1. $81 = \frac{m}{9}$

2. $h \div 3 = 12$

3. $4r = 20$

4. $34 = 17b$

In **5–12**, solve each equation.

5. $\frac{t}{35} = 42$

6. $1 = \frac{u}{2}$

7. $7s = 245$

8. $600a = 2{,}400$

9. $936 = 78p$

10. $29 = k \div 5$

11. $16d = 2{,}864$

12. $180 = \frac{g}{12}$

In **13** and **14**, write a division equation and a multiplication
equation to represent each problem.

13. Gillian read 3,135 words in 19 minutes.
Let w represent the number of words
read each minute. If Gillian read the same
number of words each minute, how many
words did she read in 1 minute?

14. Colin is a math tutor. He charges the same
amount, s, for every tutoring session. After
21 sessions he has earned $1,575. How much
does Colin charge for one tutoring session?

In **15–17**, solve each division equation and use a multiplication
equation to check your answer.

15. $9{,}522 \div 9 = k$

16. $7{,}848 \div w = 36$

17. $56{,}259 \div 57 = i$

18. Model with Math The 46 golf balls in Stavin's
golf bag have 15,180 dimples on them. Each
golf ball has the same number of dimples.
Use the bar diagram to write and solve an
equation to find the number of dimples on
each ball in Stavin's bag.

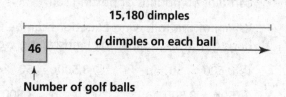

15,180 dimples

d dimples on each ball

46

↑
Number of golf balls

19. Model with Math Teddy is seven times older than Bella. If Teddy is 42 years old, how old is Bella? Write an equation to solve for Bella's age.

20. A cheese farmer distributes 672 ounces of cheese each day. The cheese is packaged in 16-ounce containers. Find the number of containers of cheese distributed each day by solving the equation $16c = 672$.

21. Reasoning On a calm day, the 32 windmills on the Bosley family wind farm each complete 120 revolutions every minute. Which operation would you use to find the total number of revolutions the 32 windmills complete in 1 minute? Explain.

22. The Columbus Junior Soccer League is selling raffle tickets to raise money for new uniforms and equipment. So far, league members have earned $1,218 from selling 84 tickets. Use the equation $1,218 \div 84 = r$ to find the cost of each raffle ticket. Then use the answer to find what the total earnings will be after 90 raffle tickets have been sold.

23. Higher Order Thinking Stanley bought 108 feet of fencing to put around his backyard. The backyard is a square. Write an equation to find the dimensions of his backyard. Is the area big enough for a pool that is 800 ft^2? Explain.

24. There are 45 houses in Grey's Lake subdivision. Each house uses 400 gallons of water each day. Write a division equation to represent the total number of gallons of water used daily in Grey's Lake subdivision.

✅ Assessment Practice

25. In May, a landscaping crew used 8,500 pounds of potting soil. One bag contains 50 pounds of potting soil.

Which of the following equations can be used to find how many bags of potting soil, p, the landscaping crew used in May?

Ⓐ $8,500 \times 50 = p$ 　　Ⓒ $8,500p = 50$

Ⓑ $50p = 8,500$ 　　　　Ⓓ $50 \div p = 8,500$

Name: _____

4-5 Additional Practice

Leveled Practice In 1–12, solve each equation.

1. $t \div 5.4 = 9.01$

$t \div 5.4 \times \boxed{} = 9.01 \times \boxed{}$

$t = \boxed{}$

2. $\frac{3}{4}x = 2$

$\frac{4}{3} \cdot \dfrac{\boxed{}}{\boxed{}} x = \boxed{} \cdot \frac{4}{3}$

$x = \dfrac{\boxed{}}{\boxed{}} \cdot \frac{4}{3}$

$x = \boxed{}$ or $2\frac{2}{3}$

3. $s + \frac{1}{4} = 12\frac{1}{2}$

4. $2\frac{2}{3} + y = 4\frac{1}{4}$

5. $a - 4\frac{3}{8} = 2\frac{1}{2}$

6. $\frac{2}{7}q = 3$

7. $9\frac{1}{12} = \frac{k}{9}$

8. $k + 24.75 = 36.12$

9. $12.85 = x - 4.34$

10. $15.95 = 3.19n$

11. $t - \frac{2}{3} = \frac{5}{6}$

12. $\frac{7}{10}c = 4\frac{1}{5}$

13. In a 400-meter relay race, 4 runners pass a baton as each of them runs 100 meters of the race. The table shows the split times for the first 3 runners of a relay team. Suppose the team has set a goal of running the race in 210 seconds. Solve the equation $(53.715 + 51.3 + 52.62) + n = 210$ to find the number of seconds, n, within which the 4th runner must finish for the team to meet its goal.

400-Meter Relay Team Split Times (seconds)	
1st runner	53.715
2nd runner	51.3
3rd runner	52.62
4th runner	n

In 14–16, use the recipe.

14. **Be Precise** Sam needs a bowl to mix her punch. She has a 2-cup bowl, a 4-cup bowl, and a 6-cup bowl. What is the smallest bowl Sam can use to make her punch? Explain.

Sam's Fruit Party Punch	
$\frac{2}{3}$ cup	Pineapple juice
$\frac{1}{2}$ cup	Orange juice
$\frac{3}{4}$ cup	Lemon/lime juice
$\frac{1}{3}$ cup	Ginger ale

15. The recipe makes 1 serving of punch. If Sam used 2 cups of pineapple juice to make her punch, how many servings did she make? Use the equation $\frac{2}{3}m = 2$ to find the number of servings.

16. Sam needs $7\frac{1}{2}$ cups of orange juice to make punch for a group of her friends. She only has $5\frac{1}{3}$ cups. Write and solve an equation to represent how many more cups of orange juice Sam needs.

17. **Model with Math** The winning team in a 400-meter relay race had a time of 198.608 seconds. Suppose all 4 of the split times were the same. Write and solve an equation to find the split times.

18. **Use Structure** Teresa placed parentheses in the expression below so that its value was greater than 80. Write the expression to show where Teresa might have placed the parentheses.

$$10.5 + 9.5 \times 3 - 1 \times 2.5$$

19. There are 6 people seated, equally spaced, along a counter. If each person has $1\frac{7}{8}$ feet of counter space, how long is the counter? Tell how you can check that your answer is reasonable.

20. **Higher Order Thinking** A bus left New York City and arrived in Philadelphia after $2\frac{1}{3}$ hours. From there, it took $1\frac{3}{4}$ hours to travel to Baltimore. It took another $\frac{5}{6}$ hour to go from Baltimore to Washington. If the bus arrived in Washington at 10:05 P.M., at what time did it leave New York City? Explain.

✓ Assessment Practice

21. Which value for y makes the equation $y \div 2.5 = 1.95$ true?

    Ⓐ $y = 0.78$ Ⓒ $y = 48.75$

    Ⓑ $y = 4.875$ Ⓓ $y = 4,875$

22. Which value for x makes the equation $x - 4.21 = 6.047$ true?

    Ⓐ $x = 10.68$ Ⓒ $x = 10.247$

    Ⓑ $x = 10.257$ Ⓓ $x = 1.837$

4-6 Additional Practice

In 1–14, write an inequality for each situation.

1. The number of students the bus holds, *s*, is less than 40.

2. The weight limit, *w*, on the bridge is 12 tons.

3. The distance, *d*, is at least 110 miles.

4. The depth of the swimming pool, *d*, cannot be deeper than $3\frac{1}{2}$ feet.

5. The least amount of water, *w*, that hikers must bring is 30 ounces.

6. The fewest number of minutes, *m*, that a player must practice per day is 45 minutes.

7. Tim's age, *t*, is not 21 years old.

8. The cost, *c*, is less than $45.

9. The length of the driveway, *d*, is longer than $\frac{1}{5}$ mile.

10. The height of the sunflower, *s*, is not $45\frac{5}{6}$ inches tall.

11. A person's height, *h*, must be at least 48 inches tall to go on this ride.

12. Leonard submitted *p* photographs in an art show. He did not submit 5 photographs.

13. Gabe has 6 more baseball cards than football cards. He has fewer than 125 baseball cards. Write an inequality for the number of football cards, *f*, he has.

14. If the sub shop sells at least 35 subs in a day, they make a profit. Write an inequality for the number of subs, *s*, they must sell in a day to make a profit.

15. Be Precise A test has 50 questions, with 25 questions worth 1 point each and 25 questions worth 3 points each. Julia had no more than 20 points subtracted from the total possible points. Write an inequality that shows the possible points, p, that Julia earned.

16. You are making gluten-free baked goods for a bake sale. One type of gluten-free flour costs $7 for a 3-pound bag. You can spend at most $28. Let n be the number of 3-pound bags of gluten-free flour you can buy. Write an inequality that represents the situation.

17. Higher Order Thinking In 4th grade, Richard read 37 books. In 5th grade, he read 9 more books than the year before. This year, in 6th grade, Richard plans to read at least 12 more books than the total number of books read in both 4th and 5th grades. Richard writes the inequality $b \geq 180$ to show the total number of books he will have read in 4th, 5th, and 6th grades. Is his inequality correct? Why or why not?

18. The waste-to-energy process generates energy in the form of electricity, heat, or fuel from the incineration of waste. Converting non-recyclable waste materials into electricity, heat, or fuel generates a renewable energy source. The 86 waste-to-energy facilities in the United States have the capacity to produce 2,720 megawatts of power per year by processing more than 28 million tons of waste per year. Write an inequality to show the possible power, p, that the waste-to-energy facilities in the United States are capable of producing.

✓ Assessment Practice

19. The Cruz family shares a family cell phone plan. The plan is for 3,200 cell phone minutes each month. The father has used 1,200 minutes. The mother has used at least 600 minutes. The two children have used 675 minutes each.

Write an inequality that shows the number of minutes the Cruz family has used. Explain.

4-7 Additional Practice

Scan for Multimedia

In **1–4**, write the inequality that each graph represents.

1.
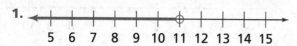

2.
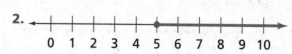

3.
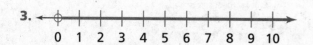

4.
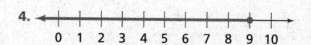

In **5 and 6**, graph each inequality on a number line.

5. $x < 7$

6. $x \geq 7$

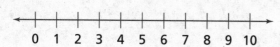

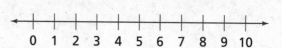

In **7 and 8**, substitute each given value of the variable to find which, if any, is a solution of the inequality.

7. $x < 12$ $x = 12.5, 13.5, 22, 112$

8. $y > 23$ $y = 20, 23, 25.1, 35$

In **9–16**, give three solutions of each inequality.

9. $x < 9$ **10.** $x < 6$ **11.** $y > 2$ **12.** $y \geq 100$

13. $z < 8$ **14.** $x \geq 77$ **15.** $u > 10.9$ **16.** $u \leq 13.99$

17. At the right is a portion of the menu at a diner. The inequality $m < 5$ represents the amount of money, m, that Elizabeth has to spend on lunch at the diner. Which items can she choose for lunch?

Diner Menu	
Turkey Sandwich	$3.99
Tuna Sandwich with Fruit	$5.45
Italian Beef Sandwich	$4.75
Slice of Cheese Pizza	$2.25
Grilled Chicken Sandwich	$6.00

18. **Use Structure** The graph on the number line below represents the solutions of the inequality $y < 6$. How many solutions are there? Write three of the solutions that are greater than 5.

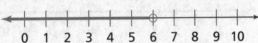

19. **Reasoning** Graph the inequalities $x > 3$ and $x \leq 4$ on the same number line. What value, if any, is not a solution of either inequality?

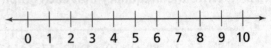

20. **Higher Order Thinking** The width of a youth soccer field must be at least 45 meters, but it cannot exceed 60 meters. Write two inequalities that describe the width, w, of a youth soccer field. Then write two integers that are solutions of both inequalities.

21. The inequality $p \geq 4$ describes the number of pounds of apples, p, Bill needs when he is making apple strudel. Can a total weight of either 3.5 pounds or 4 pounds be enough for Bill to make apple strudel? Explain.

22. Jeremiah spends at least $14.50 on dinner every day. Write an inequality to represent the amount Jeremiah spends. Then write two examples of amounts Jeremiah might spend.

23. Payton did not spend $15.00 at the grocery store. Write an inequality to represent the amount Payton spent. Then write two examples of amounts Payton might have spent.

✓ Assessment Practice

24. Select all the given values of z that make the inequality $4z > 17$ true.

   ☐ 4
   ☐ 4.25
   ☐ 5
   ☐ 5.25
   ☐ 6

25. Tricia started a graph to show the inequality $x \geq 12$. Finish labeling the number line and draw the graph.

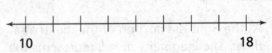

4-8 Additional Practice

Scan for
Multimedia

In 1–8, identify the independent variable and the dependent variable in each situation.

1. The number of hours, *h*, spent studying and the score, *s*, on a test

2. The length, *l*, of a pencil and the number of times, *t*, it has been sharpened

3. The length of a story in pages, *p*, and the number of words, *w*, in a story

4. The number of students, *s*, ahead of you in the lunch line and the time, *t*, it takes you to get lunch

5. The amount of time, *t*, to finish a race and the number of laps, *l*, around a track

6. Tickets, *t*, sold for a race and the amount of money, *m*, collected

7. The length, *l*, of a fence and the amount of wood, *w*, to make the fence

8. The height, *h*, of a fence and the time, *t*, it takes to climb the fence

9. Write your own situation in which speed, *s*, is an independent variable.

10. Name at least two independent variables that could result in a change in a monthly cell phone bill.

11. **Critique Reasoning** You spend *d* dollars for *g* identical pairs of glasses. A friend claims that because *d* increases if you increase *g*, and *g* increases if you increase *d*, either *d* or *g* could be the independent variable. Is your friend correct? Explain.

12. The cost, *c*, of supplies for school depends on other factors. List at least two independent variables that could affect the cost of school supplies.

13. **Reasoning** Two friends hiked the Appalachian Trail from Georgia to Maine. List at least two independent variables that could affect the number of days they took to hike the trail.

Katahdin, Maine

Appalachian Trail: 2,181 miles long

Springer Mountain, Georgia

14. Steve had *s* songs on his music player. He bought *n* new songs. What is the dependent variable? Explain.

15. **Construct Arguments** A baseball team gets 3 outs for each inning it comes up to bat. So far this season, Silvio's team has batted in 45 innings, *n*, and has made 135 outs, *t*. What is the dependent variable? Explain.

16. **Vocabulary** Identify the *independent variable* and the *dependent variable* in the situation below.

   The number of laps you swim, *s*, and the time, *t*, you spend swimming.

17. **Higher Order Thinking** Ivan says that length, *l*, can be used as either an independent or a dependent variable. Give an example in which length, *l*, is a dependent variable. Then describe another situation in which it is an independent variable.

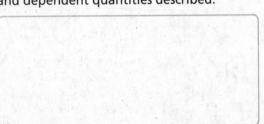

Assessment Practice

18. The cost of a hamburger at a restaurant and the size of the hamburger are related quantities.

   PART A

   Use variables to represent the independent and dependent quantities described.

   PART B

   Use variables to represent the dependent variable and the independent variable in this sentence: *The owner of Arlo's Hamburger Hut records the total income from hamburger sales and the total number of hamburgers sold.*

4-9 Additional Practice

Scan for Multimedia

In 1–4, write a rule and an equation that represents the pattern in each table.

1.

x	3	6	11	13	15
y	5	8	13	15	17

2.

x	2	5	6	8	9
y	6	15	18	24	27

3.

x	4	12	20	36	40
y	1	3	5	9	10

4.

x	5	7	9	10	12
y	0	2	4	5	7

In 5–8, use the equation to complete each table.

5. $y = 3x + 7$

x	0	1	2	3
y				

6. $y = 4x - 4$

x	2	4	6	8
y				

7. $y = 2x + 7$

x	1	3	5	7
y				

8. $y = \frac{1}{4}x + 5$

x	0	4	8	12
y				

9. Complete the table to show a pattern. Then write a rule and an equation for the pattern.

x				
y				

10. Explain how you would find the pattern in this table and how you would write a rule and an equation for the pattern.

x	4	5	7	10	12
y	0	1	3	6	8

11. Grace has $100. She is buying charms for her bracelet that cost $5 each. Write an equation showing the relationship between the number of charms, c, she buys and the amount of money she has left, m.

12. Use the equation you wrote for Exercise 11 to find the number of charms Grace can buy before she runs out of money.

In **13** and **14**, use the table.

13. **Reasoning** The Gadget Factory sells winkydiddles. The table shows the cost, c, of w winkydiddles. If each winkydiddle costs the same amount, what is the price of each winkydiddle?

Number of Winkydiddles, w	7	12	26	31
Cost, c	$24.50	$42.00	$91.00	$108.50

14. Write an equation that can be used to find c, the cost of w winkydiddles.

In **15** and **16**, write an equation that describes the pattern in each table.

15.

x	4	6	8	10	12
y	11	13	15	17	19

16.

x	5	6	7	10	11	12
y	2.5	3	3.5	5	5.5	6

In **17** and **18**, the equation $\ell = 3w$ represents that the length, ℓ, of a rectangle is 3 times its width, w.

17. **Model with Math** Create a table to show the length of the rectangle when its width is 1, 2, 3, 5, and 8 units.

18. **Higher Order Thinking** How could you use the equation $p = 2\ell + 2w$ to find the perimeter, p, of the rectangle when its width, w, is 15?

19. The table shows the total cost for the number of raffle tickets purchased. Write an equation that represents the relationship between these two quantities. Use the equation to find the cost of 6 tickets.

Number of Tickets	5	8	10	11
Cost	$417.50	$668	$835	$918.50

PRACTICE **TUTORIAL**

4-10 Additional Practice

Scan for
Multimedia

In 1 and 2, complete the table and the graph to show the relationship between the variables in each equation.

1. Bodie drew a triangle. The base of his triangle is $\frac{1}{2}$ the height of the triangle.
Let h = height.
Let b = base.
Graph $b = \frac{h}{2}$.

$b = \frac{h}{2}$	
h	b
1	☐
2	☐
☐	☐

2. Eva's mother will add $5 to all other donations that she collects for the school fund drive.

Let a = all other donations.
Let t = total donations.
Graph $t = a + 5$.

$t = a + 5$	
a	t
10	☐
20	☐
☐	☐

In 3 and 4, use the information about the femur bone.

3. Forensic anthropologists analyze skeletons to help solve crimes. They can use the length of a femur bone to estimate the height of a skeleton. The height of a skeleton is about 30 inches taller than twice the length of the femur bone. Let h represent the height of a skeleton. Let f represent the length of a femur bone. Write an equation to represent the height of a skeleton.

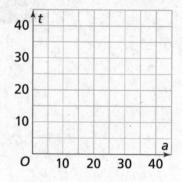

Adult femur bones are often between 15 and 20 inches long.

4. Higher Order Thinking Rhonda is 5 feet tall. About how long is her femur? Explain.

In 5–8, use the picture at the right.

5. People get energy from the food they eat. This energy is measured in calories. When you exercise, you use up or burn calories. The picture at the right shows about how many calories a 125-pound person burns each minute bowling. How many calories does a 125-pound person burn in 2 hours of bowling?

3 calories burned each minute

6. **Model with Math** Use the information from Exercise 5 to write an equation representing the number of calories burned each minute while bowling. Let *m* represent the number of minutes a 125-pound person bowls. Let *c* represent the number of calories burned.

7. Complete the table for the equation you wrote in Exercise 6.

m	c

8. Complete the graph using the table data from Exercise 7.

✓ Assessment Practice

9. A Florida manatee weighs 60 pounds at birth.

PART A

Write an equation that describes the relationship shown in the table on the right.

Number of weeks, w	Weight in pounds, p
0	60
2	80
4	100

PART B

Describe the relationship between the variables in the table and the equation.

5-1 Additional Practice

In **1–6**, use the shapes shown below. Write a ratio for each comparison in three ways.

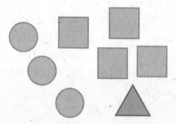

1. The number of triangles to the total number of shapes

2. The number of squares to the number of triangles

3. The number of triangles to the number of squares

4. The number of triangles to the number of circles

5. The number of circles to the total number of shapes

6. The total number of shapes to the number of squares

In **7–10**, draw a diagram to help solve each problem.

7. A cleaning crew can clean 5 offices in 6 hours. How many offices can they clean in 12 hours?

8. Joseph is planting a vegetable garden. He plants 2 tomato plants for every 5 pepper plants. If Joseph plants 14 tomato plants, how many pepper plants does he plant?

9. There are 4 adult chaperones for every 15 students who attend a school field trip. If there were 135 students, how many adults would there be on the field trip?

10. Ms. Dawson spent $28 for 8 notebooks. If each notebook sells for the same price, how much would she have to spend for 48 notebooks?

11. There are 14 boys and 16 girls in Mr. Allen's class. What is the ratio of girls to the total number of students in the class? Write the ratio in 3 ways.

12. A pet store keeps 4 small fish in every 10 gallons of water. How many gallons of water are needed for 36 fish?

13. Gary has 24 quarters, 16 dimes, and 32 pennies. Write a ratio that compares the combined number of dimes and pennies to the number of quarters.

14. Reasoning There are 12 students who play the clarinet and 16 students who play the viola. What does the ratio 16:12 describe?

15. Be Precise An orchard contains 12 rows of Granny Smith apple trees, 10 rows of Fuji apple trees, 15 rows of Gala apple trees, 2 rows of Golden Delicious apple trees, and 2 rows of Jonathan apple trees. Write each ratio in three ways.

   a. Rows of Gala apple trees to Granny Smith apple trees

   b. Rows of Fuji apple trees to the total number of rows of apple trees

16. Higher Order Thinking Lori is 6 years old. In three years, her cousin Philip will be twice as old as Lori will be. Write the ratio of Philip's age now to Lori's age now.

17. The ratio of desktop computers to laptop computers at a company is 2 to 9. If there were 108 laptop computers, how many computers would there be in all at the company?

☑ Assessment Practice

18. A company makes uniforms for a fast-food restaurant. The diagram below represents the relationship between the number of yards of blue fabric and the number of yards of white fabric used.

What is the ratio of the number of yards of blue fabric to the number of yards of white fabric?

Ⓐ 8 : 5

Ⓑ 8 : 8

Ⓒ 8 : 13

Ⓓ 8 : 21

Yards of Blue Fabric

0   8   16   24   32   40   48

0   13   26   39   52   65   78

Yards of White Fabric

5-2 Additional Practice

In **1–9**, write three ratios that are equivalent to the given ratio.

1. $\frac{3}{5}$

2. $\frac{4}{8}$

3. $\frac{6}{18}$

4. 8:10

5. 6:8

6. 10:12

7. 12 to 18

8. 16 to 18

9. 5 to 25

In **10–15**, use = or ≠ to show whether the ratios are equivalent.

10. 3:12 ◯ 6:24

11. $\frac{28}{16}$ ◯ $\frac{7}{4}$

12. 4 to 20 ◯ 1 to 4

13. $\frac{4}{6}$ ◯ $\frac{6}{9}$

14. 27 to 9 ◯ 24 to 4

15. 6:10 ◯ 8:15

In **16** and **17**, complete the tables with equivalent ratios.

16. A wildlife conservancy maintains a ratio of 2 squirrels for every 8 birds. How many birds would there be if there were 15 squirrels?

Animals					
Squirrels	2	4	5		15
Birds	8		20	40	

17. At Rolling Hills Middle School, the ratio of the total number of students to the number of students with pets is 3 to 1. If there are 243 students at the school, how many students have pets?

Number of Students with Pets	1	3	9		81
Total Number of Students	3	9		81	

18. Scientists study ways to increase the population of wild salmon. How many salmon eggs may be needed to produce 18 adult salmon?

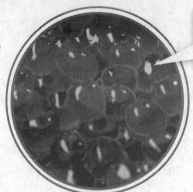

For every 8,000 eggs, only 2 adults may survive.

19. Construct Arguments Tell why you cannot multiply or divide by 0 to find equivalent ratios.

20. Critique Reasoning Dale says the ratios 3:5 and 2:10 are equivalent. Is he correct? Explain.

21. Is the ratio of length to width equivalent for these two rectangles? Explain.

12 in.

8 in.

20 in.

16 in.

22. Higher Order Thinking An animal shelter can hold a total of 60 cats and dogs. For every 5 cats the shelter can house, there is room for 7 dogs. How many cats and dogs are at the shelter when it is completely full?

23. Be Precise For a small music concert, each child in attendance will get a free toy trumpet. Five adults are expected for every 2 children. Find how many children are expected if there are 15 adults, 25 adults, and 40 adults.

✓ Assessment Practice

24. In a section of a lake, there are 8 sailboats for every 6 motorboats. Complete the table to find equivalent ratios and determine the number of sailboats there will be when there are 24 motorboats.

Sailboats	8			
Motorboats	6	12	18	24

25. Which ratios represent Pi (π)? Select all that apply.

☐ 66 : 21

☐ 60 : 20

☐ 45 : 15

☐ 22 : 7

☐ 21 : 7

5-3 Additional Practice

 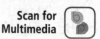

1. Edith and Rashida are shooting free throws. Complete the ratio tables. Who has a better ratio of baskets to shots?

Edith

Baskets	1			4	5
Shots	3	6	9		

Rashida

Baskets	2			8	10
Shots	5	10	15		

2. In Mrs. Washington's class, there are 2 students in band for every 3 students in chorus. In Mr. Utley's class there are 5 students in band for every 7 students in chorus. Complete the ratio tables. Which class has a greater ratio of students in band to students in chorus?

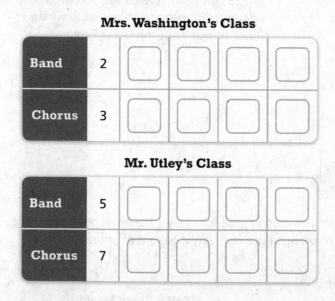

Mrs. Washington's Class

Band	2				
Chorus	3				

Mr. Utley's Class

Band	5				
Chorus	7				

3. Aiko has 5 shirts for every 3 pairs of pants. Her brother Haro has 7 shirts for every 4 pairs of pants. Complete the ratio tables. Which sibling has a greater ratio of shirts to pants?

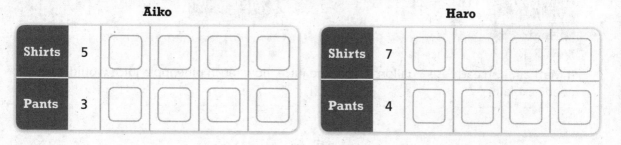

Aiko

Shirts	5			
Pants	3			

Haro

Shirts	7			
Pants	4			

In 4 and 5, complete the ratio tables to solve the problems.

4. **Model with Math** Every 5 days during the week, Morgan sleeps 40 hours. How many days would it take him to sleep 200 hours?

Morgan's Sleep Ratio Table

Days					
Hours of Sleep					

5. **Reasoning** Alice sleeps 50 hours every 6 days. Does Alice or Morgan have a greater days to hours of sleep ratio? Explain.

Alice's Sleep Ratio Table

Days					
Hours of Sleep					

6. Mrs. Henderson has 16 boys in her class of 24 students. Mr. Gregory has 18 boys in his class of 30 students. Which class has the greater ratio of boys to students? Explain.

7. **Higher Order Thinking** Jacob and Jordan are training for track season. Jacob did 39 sit-ups in 30 seconds. Jordan did 59 sit-ups in 50 seconds. Who will likely do more sit-ups in $2\frac{1}{2}$ minutes? Explain.

☑ Assessment Practice

8. Jan makes a party punch that requires 2 gallons of orange juice for every $\frac{1}{2}$ gallon of pineapple juice. Matt's party punch recipe calls for 3 gallons of orange juice for every 2 gallons of pineapple juice.

PART A

Complete the tables using the given ratios.

Jan's Party Punch

Orange Juice (gal)	2		6	
Pineapple Juice (gal)	$\frac{1}{2}$	1		2

Matt's Party Punch

Orange Juice (gal)	3	6		12
Pineapple Juice (gal)	2		6	

PART B

If Matt and Jan each use 6 gallons of orange juice, how much pineapple juice would each need? Explain.

Name: _____

5-4 Additional Practice

Scan for
Multimedia

In **1** and **2**, complete each table. Then label the coordinates along the
y-axis and plot the pairs of values on the coordinate plane.

1.

2	4	6	8	10
3				

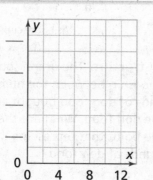

2.

1	2	3	4	5
2				

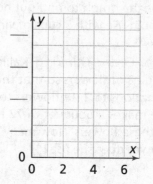

---

3. A store charges $140 for every 10 bags of fertilizer a farmer buys.

a. Complete the table. Graph the values.

Fertilizer (bags)	10		30	40	
Cost ($)	140	280			840

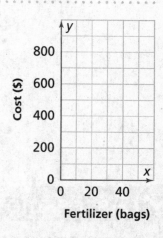

b. How much would a farmer pay for 50 bags of fertilizer? Explain.

---

4. A car uses 5 gallons of gas for every 120 miles it travels.

a. Complete the table. Graph the values.

Gas (gal)	5		20
Distance (mi)	120	360	

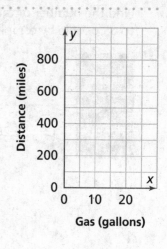

b. How many gallons of gas does the car use if it travels 600 miles?

c. How far can the car travel if it uses 30 gallons of gas?

5. Gavin makes a homemade cleaner using $\frac{1}{2}$ cup vinegar for every 2 quarts of water.

a. Complete the table. Graph the values.

Vinegar (c)	$\frac{1}{2}$	☐	$1\frac{1}{2}$	☐
Water (qt)	2	4	☐	8

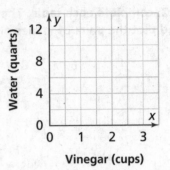

b. Use the graph to find out how much water Gavin would use with 3 cups of vinegar.

6. **Higher Order Thinking** Kallie makes bouquets of flowers so that the ratios are 4 carnations to 2 sunflowers to 3 lilies. Kallie makes a bouquet of 72 flowers using only these flowers. How many of each type of flower does she use?

7. **Use Structure** The graph shows the relationship between the number of pounds of dog food bought and the cost of the dog food. What are the coordinates of the point that represents the cost of 6 pounds of dog food?

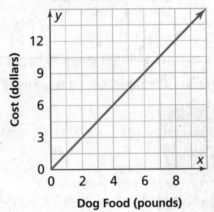

Dog Food (pounds)

✓ Assessment Practice

8. A restaurant pushes together 3 tables to seat 13 people.

PART A

Find the number of tables needed to seat up to 65 people by completing the ratio table.

Tables	3	☐	9	12	☐
People	13	26	☐	☐	65

PART B

Graph the pairs of values.

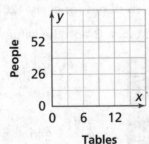

Tables

5-5 Additional Practice

Scan for
Multimedia

In 1 and 2, write each statement as a rate.

1. Jon buys 3 shirts for $20.

2. Brenda records 76 songs on 4 albums.

In 3 and 4, find the value of m.

3.

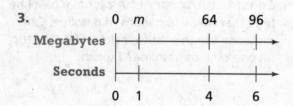

4.

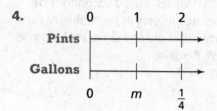

In 5–8, find the unit rate.

5. $\dfrac{121 \text{ meals}}{11 \text{ days}}$

6. $\dfrac{50 \text{ min}}{20 \text{ calls}}$

7. $\dfrac{91 \text{ books}}{7 \text{ weeks}}$

8. $\dfrac{1,275 \text{ ants}}{5 \text{ anthills}}$

In 9 and 10, complete each table.

9.

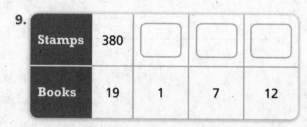

Stamps	380			
Books	19	1	7	12

10.

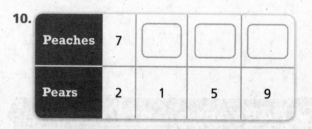

Peaches	7			
Pears	2	1	5	9

11. It took Perla 8 games to score 30 points. At that rate, how many games will it take her to score 45 points?

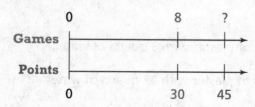

12. A shark can chase prey at about 30 miles per hour. What is this rate in miles per minute?

In 13–15, use the table.

13. Mr. Ernest wants to know how many miles he can travel with his motorcycle for each gallon of gas. What is the unit rate in miles per gallon?

Distance Driven Using 10 Gallons of Gasoline

Vehicle	Miles
Car	285
Van	140
Motorcycle	640

14. **Reasoning** Ms. Ellis used 25 gallons of gas delivering flowers in her delivery van. How many miles did she drive making the deliveries? Explain.

15. **Construct Arguments** A car has a gasoline tank that holds 18 gallons of gasoline. Can someone use this car to make a 500-mile trip on one tank of gasoline? Explain.

16. **Higher Order Thinking** This Venn diagram shows the relationship of ratios to rates to unit rates. Describe a real-world situation involving a ratio relationship. Then write the ratio as 2 different equivalent rates and as a unit rate.

Ratios

Rates

Unit Rates

☑ Assessment Practice

17. A potter mixes 6 pounds of pottery plaster with 2 quarts of water.
Select all the statements that are true.

☐ $\frac{3 \text{ lb plaster}}{1 \text{ qt water}}$ is a unit rate for the mix.

☐ $\frac{3 \text{ qt water}}{1 \text{ lb plaster}}$ is a unit rate for the mix.

☐ Using the same rate, the potter mixes 9 pounds of plaster with 3 quarts of water.

☐ Using the same rate, the potter mixes 4 pounds of plaster with 12 quarts of water.

☐ Using the same rate, the potter mixes 12 pounds of plaster with 4 quarts of water.

5-6 Additional Practice

Scan for
Multimedia

In 1–4, find each unit price.

1. 8 pencils for $2.24

2. 5 used books for $9.45

3. $\frac{1}{2}$ gallon of orange juice for $3.65

4. 6 goldfish for $7.38

In 5–8, determine which is the better value.

5. 1 pound of apples for $2.15 or 3 pounds of apples for $5.76

6. 8 bungee cords for $10.00 or 20 bungee cords for $22.00

7. 32 fluid ounces of juice for $7.04 or 20 fluid ounces of juice for $4.80

8. 5 ounces of insect repellant for $6.95 or 14 ounces of insect repellant for $19.60

In 9–11, compare the rates to find which is greater.

9. 510 visitors in 30 hours or 960 visitors in 60 hours

10. 660 miles on 20 gallons or 850 miles on 25 gallons

11. 1,080 labels on 90 sheets or 2,250 labels on 150 sheets

In 12–14, compare the rates to find which is the better value.

12. $285 for 150 ft^2 of carpet or $252 for 120 ft^2 of carpet

13. $74 for 4 theater tickets or $91 for 5 theater tickets

14. $960 for 30 textbooks or $1,625 for 50 textbooks

15. **Reasoning** Which box of cereal is a better value? Explain.

16. **Construct Arguments** Ruth is buying potatoes. Which is a better value: a 4-pound bag for $2.40 or a 10-pound bag for $5.20? Explain when a wiser purchase may **NOT** be the better value.

17. **Be Precise** On Monday, it snowed 30 inches in 16 hours. On Thursday, it snowed 21 inches in 6 hours. On which day did it snow at a greater rate each hour? How much more per hour?

18. **Higher Order Thinking** The Fleet Feet training log is shown at the right. Deana ran 462 miles. Her weekly mileage rate was greater than Pavel's rate but less than Alberto's rate. Complete the training log. How many weeks could it have taken her to run 462 miles?

Fleet Feet Training Log

Runner	Miles	Weeks	Rate per Week
Pavel	672	21	
Deana	462	?	
Alberto	420	12	

19. An office supply store sells packs of pens. Bargain shoppers have four options.

PART A

Complete the table to find the unit price for each option.

Packs of Pens	Unit Price
5 pens for $4.85	
12 pens for $11.40	
25 pens for $24.50	
60 pens for $57.60	

PART B

Compare the unit rates found in Part A and identify the best value.

5-7 Additional Practice

Scan for
Multimedia

In 1–3, solve the rate problems.

1. Jason and his family travel 160 miles in 3.2 hours. If they continue at this constant speed, how long will it take them to travel 300 miles? Complete the table.

   It will take Jason and his family ☐ hours to travel 300 miles.

Time (hours)	Distance (miles)
1	☐
3.2	160
☐	300

2. A space shuttle orbits Earth at a rate of about 4,375 miles in 15 minutes. At this rate, how far does the space shuttle travel around Earth in 1 hour?

3. A store sells 4 cans of beans for $9. What is the price of 7 cans of beans?

4. The new *Vigo the Vampire Hunter* novel is 520 pages. Skyler has read 145 pages in 5 hours. Ramon has read 124 pages in 4 hours.

   a. Who reads faster, Skyler or Ramon?

   b. How long will it take Ramon to read the entire novel if he continues to read at his current rate? Explain.

5. Hanna and Dien are both getting a raise. Who will earn more per hour after the raise?

	Hours Worked	Earnings	Raise (per hour)
Hanna	8	$78.00	$1.00
Dien	6	$60.60	$0.50

   a. How can you use unit prices to find Hanna's and Dien's new earnings per hour? Explain.

   b. Solve the problem.

6. **Model with Math** Kenny is walking at a constant speed of 3.5 miles per hour. How far can he walk in 6 hours? Complete the table. Then write an equation to find the total distance, d, traveled after t hours to solve the problem.

Time, t (hours)	1	2	3	4
Distance, d (miles)	3.5			

In 7 and 8, use the picture at the right.

7. If the maglev train travels at a constant speed of 480 kilometers per hour for $\frac{1}{4}$ hour, how far does the train travel?

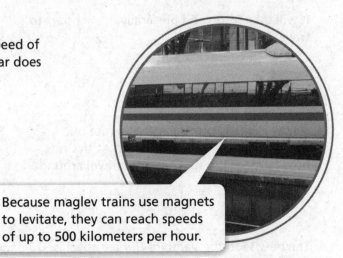

8. If the maglev train traveled at a constant rate of its top speed for 10 kilometers, what is the approximate amount of time in hours the train would have traveled?

Because maglev trains use magnets to levitate, they can reach speeds of up to 500 kilometers per hour.

9. Cora babysat for $3\frac{1}{2}$ hours and charged $28. At the same hourly rate, what would she charge for $5\frac{1}{2}$ hours of babysitting?

10. **Higher Order Thinking** A cyclist rode at a constant speed of 21 mph for 3 hours. Then she decreased her rate of speed to 17 mph for 4 hours. How far did the cyclist ride in 7 hours?

☑ Assessment Practice

11. Jack drove 325 miles in 5 hours.

PART A

How many miles per hour did Jack drive?

PART B

Jack will drive 520 more miles at the same rate. How long will it take Jack to drive the 520 miles?

Name: _____

In **1–12**, complete each conversion.

1. 5 lb = [_____] oz

2. 2.5 T = [_____] lb

3. 39 ft = [_____] yd

4. 22 pt = [_____] qt

5. 4.5 lb = [_____] oz

6. 3 qt = [_____] gal

7. 5 qt = [_____] gal

8. 13 pt = [_____] qt

9. $\frac{1}{2}$ mi = [_____] ft

10. 1.5 mi = [_____] yd

11. 17 yd = [_____] ft

12. 25,000 lb = [_____] T

13. Use an equivalent rate to convert 3 quarts to pints.

14. Use dimensional analysis to convert 9 teaspoons to tablespoons.

15. William bought a piece of wood that is 3 feet long. He cuts it into two pieces. One piece is 14 inches long. How long is the other piece?

16. Ellie needs $\frac{1}{2}$ cup of milk to make blueberry muffins. She pours $\frac{1}{2}$ cup of milk from a quart container of milk. How many cups of milk will be left in the container?

17. Tania needs to buy at least 3 pounds of bananas. If she buys a bunch of bananas that weighs 42 ounces, will she have enough? Explain.

18. A bridge has a sign that says "Maximum Weight 6 Tons." If a truck weighs 13,000 pounds, is it too heavy to cross the bridge? Explain.

In **19** and **20**, use the picture.

19. **Look for Relationships** Chris is buying material for an art project. Two stores have the material she needs. Compare prices to find which material is the better value. Explain.

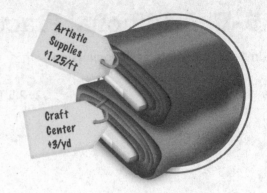

Artistic Supplies $1.25/ft

Craft Center $3/yd

20. Chris decides to buy 102 feet of the Craft Center material. What is the cost?

21. **Make Sense and Persevere** Bill is making smoothies for his friends. If 4 ounces of fruit is needed for each smoothie, how many pounds of fruit would he need to make 10 smoothies?

22. **Construct Arguments** How is converting units from cups to pints like converting units from ounces to pounds? How is it different?

23. **Higher Order Thinking** A car is traveling 25 miles per hour. What is the car's speed in feet per second? Use the conversion factors $\frac{5,280 \text{ feet}}{1 \text{ mile}}$ and $\frac{1 \text{ hour}}{3,600 \text{ seconds}}$.

24. Brian pole-vaulted over a bar that was 189 inches high. How many inches higher must he vault to go over a bar that is 16 feet high?

Assessment Practice

25. Select all the conversions that are true.

- ☐ 4 pt = 1 gal
- ☐ 8 pt = 1 gal
- ☐ 1.5 gal = 6 qt
- ☐ $1\frac{1}{2}$ gal = 8 pt
- ☐ 1.5 gal = 24 c

Customary Units

Capacity
1 tbsp = 3 tsp
1 fl oz = 2 tbsp
1 c = 8 fl oz
1 pt = 2 c
1 qt = 2 pt
1 gal = 4 qt

5-9 Additional Practice

Scan for Multimedia

In 1–12, complete each conversion.

1. 45 g = ⬚ mg

2. 3,450 mL = ⬚ L

3. 6.5 m = ⬚ mm

4. 1.68 L = ⬚ mL

5. 28 cm = ⬚ mm

6. 7,658 g = ⬚ kg

7. 600 cm = ⬚ m

8. 5,000 dg = ⬚ g

9. 5.1 km = ⬚ m

10. 0.178 L = ⬚ mL

11. 4,300 m = ⬚ km

12. 2.7 m = ⬚ cm

13. Use an equivalent rate to convert 24 centiliters to liters.

14. Use dimensional analysis to convert 0.33 kilometer to meters.

In 15–17, use the table, which shows the amounts of three items that Nobu bought at a farmer's market.

15. What is the mass of the cantaloupe in grams?

Item	Amount
Green Pepper	400 g
Cantaloupe	3 kg
Tomato	630 g

16. What is the total mass in kilograms of all the items that Nobu bought?

17. Anya bought some tomatoes with a mass of 1.2 kilograms. How much heavier are Anya's tomatoes than Nobu's tomato?

In **18–20**, use the table. *The Persistence of Memory*, by Salvador Dali, and *Water Lilies*, by Claude Monet, are two famous paintings.

18. **Be Precise** What are the length and height of *The Persistence of Memory* in centimeters?

Painting Title	Length (meters)	Height (meters)
The Persistence of Memory	0.33	0.241
Water Lilies	5.99	1.995

19. What are the length and height of *Water Lilies* in millimeters?

20. The painting *Starry Night* by Vincent Van Gogh is 92.1 centimeters long. Which painting is longer, *Starry Night* or *The Persistence of Memory*? How much longer?

21. **Construct Arguments** A banana has a mass of 122 g. Explain how to find the mass of the banana in milligrams.

22. **Higher Order Thinking** If a car is traveling at a speed of 40 kilometers per hour, what is its approximate rate in meters per minute?

23. A computer disk has a mass of 20 g. How many of these disks would you need to equal a total mass of 1 kg?

24. A chemist needs 2,220 mL of potassium chloride to complete an experiment. She has 2 L. How many more liters does she need?

✅ Assessment Practice

25. Select all the conversions that are equivalent to the length of a 725-meter suspension bridge.

☐ 725,000 mm

☐ 72,500 cm

☐ 7,250 cm

☐ 7.25 km

☐ 0.725 km

26. Select all the conversions that are equivalent to the mass of a 6.75-kilogram bowling ball.

☐ 67.5 hg

☐ 67.5 dag

☐ 6,750 g

☐ 67,500 cg

☐ 6,750,000 mg

5-10 Additional Practice

Scan for
Multimedia

In 1–9, find the equivalent measure. Round to the nearest tenth.

1. 4 in. ≈ [   ] cm

2. 12 gal ≈ [   ] L

3. 35 lb ≈ [   ] kg

4. 20 km ≈ [   ] mi

5. 125 in. ≈ [   ] m

6. 18 L ≈ [   ] qt

7. 55 oz ≈ [   ] g

8. 34 in. ≈ [   ] cm

9. 70 mi ≈ [   ] km

10. Aidan needs 15 liters of cleaning solution. He can buy a 2-gallon jug ($4.28), a 3-gallon jug ($5.92), a 4-gallon jug ($6.56), or a 7-gallon jug ($12.98). Which jug should he purchase to get at least 15 liters of cleaning solution and spend the least amount of money?

11. Elise ran 2 miles in 15 minutes. Teagan ran 3 kilometers in 15 minutes. Who ran at a faster rate? Explain.

12. Ryan is running in a 5-kilometer race. How many feet will he run in the race? Use the conversion rates 5,280 ft = 1 mi and 1 mi ≈ 1.61 km. Round to the nearest hundred feet.

13. Luisa bought 4.4 kilograms of apples. How many ounces of apples did she buy? Use the conversion rates 1 kilogram ≈ 2.20 pounds and 1 pound = 16 ounces. Round to the nearest ounce.

14. Enzo needs to buy some sand for his sandbox. He can either buy a 10-pound bag of sand for $18 or a 6-kilogram bag of sand for $20.

a. Which is a better value? Explain.

b. If Enzo needs 18 pounds of sand, what should he buy so that he spends the least amount of money overall? Explain.

15. Critique Reasoning A recipe Carmen is making calls for 4 cups of milk. She has 1 liter of milk. Her sister says she has enough milk. Is her sister correct? Explain.

Units of Capacity Conversion Chart	
1 pt = 2 c	1 gal ≈ 3.79 L
1 qt = 2 pt	1 qt ≈ 0.95 L
1 gal = 4 qt	

16. Which car gets better mileage: a car that gets 23 miles per gallon or a car that gets 45 kilometers per gallon?

17. Be Precise Keiko is using metric units of capacity to find an equivalent measure for 3 gallons. She records the liquid volume using milliliters and deciliters. Which unit will give a more precise measure? Explain.

18. Make Sense and Persevere A 1-mile race is 5,280 feet long. To the nearest tenth, about how many meters are there in 1 mile? Explain.

19. Higher Order Thinking Six juice boxes have a total liquid volume of 48 fluid ounces. There are 8 fluid ounces in 1 cup. There are about 4.23 cups in 1 liter. About how many liters are there in 48 fluid ounces? Round your answer to the nearest tenth.

✓ Assessment Practice

20. A gorilla has a mass of 156 kilograms. Select all the customary measures that are less than 156 kilograms.

- ☐ 400 lb
- ☐ 350 lb
- ☐ 300 lb
- ☐ 250 lb
- ☐ 200 lb

21. The public library has a mural that measures 15 meters wide. Select all the customary measures that are greater than 15 meters.

- ☐ 500 in.
- ☐ 550 in.
- ☐ 600 in.
- ☐ 45 ft
- ☐ 50 ft

6-1 Additional Practice

In 1–3, write the percent of each figure that is shaded.

1.

2.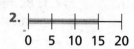

3.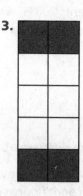

In 4–6, shade each model to represent the given percent.

4. 3%

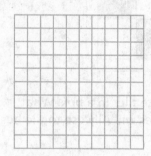

5. 80%

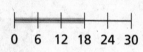

6. 30%

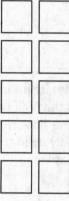

7. Jana divided a sheet of paper into 5 equal sections and colored 2 of the sections red. What percent of the paper did she color?

8. **Model with Math** Water makes up about 60% of the average adult's body weight. Represent this percent by shading in the squares.

9. **Reasoning** Kelly saved $150. That is 50% of the money she earned this summer. How much did Kelly earn this summer?

10. When students were asked to name their favorite type of music, 3 out of every 5 students chose rock music. What percent of the students chose another type of music?

In 11 and 12, use the line segment.

B •————————————————————• C
             8 cm

11. If $\overline{BC}$ represents 200%, what is the length of a line segment that is 75%? Explain.

12. If $\overline{BC}$ represents 10%, what is the length of a line segment that is 100%? Explain.

- -

In 13–15, use the diagram at the right.

13. Make Sense and Persevere Ally wants to tile her laundry room floor with checkered ceramic tiles as shown. What percent of Ally's floor will be white?

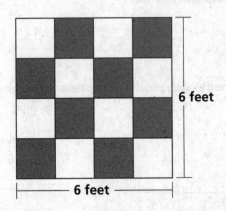

6 feet

6 feet

14. Higher Order Thinking Ally buys a box of blue tiles that will cover 18 ft². What percent of the floor can she tile using this box? Does Ally need to buy another box of blue tiles? Explain.

15. There are 25 white tiles in a box. What percent of the tiles will Ally use to tile her laundry room floor?

☑ **Assessment Practice**

16. Select all the figures that are shaded to represent 75% of the whole.

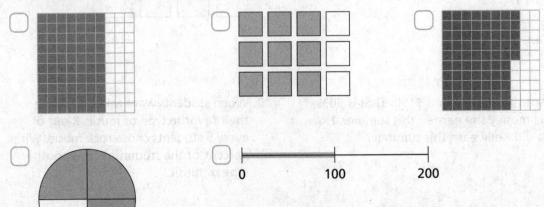

0   100   200

6-2 Additional Practice

Scan for Multimedia

In **1–9**, write each number in two equivalent forms as a fraction, a decimal, or a percent.

1. 0.24

2. $\frac{2}{100}$

3. 16%

4. 0.43

5. 18%

6. $\frac{1}{8}$

7. $\frac{1}{4}$

8. 5%

9. $\frac{3}{8}$

In **10–15**, use the circle graphs.

10. Reasoning What decimal shows the combined portion of boys who like pop and country music?

11. What type of music did $\frac{1}{5}$ of the girls choose as their favorite?

12. Which types of music are the favorites for the most boys? Write the percent of each as a fraction.

13. Which type of music is the least favorite music for the girls? What is that percent as a decimal?

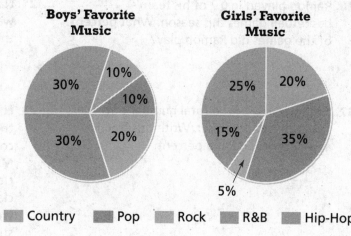

Boys' Favorite Music

Girls' Favorite Music

Country   Pop   Rock   R&B   Hip-Hop

14. Which two types of the girls' favorite music combined represent 0.45? Write each percent as a fraction.

15. Which types of music are the boys' least favorite? Write each percent as a fraction and a decimal.

16. Two out of every 5 customers at a restaurant use cash to pay for their meal. What percent of the customers pay with cash?

17. Enrollment in French class at a high school is 0.72 of enrollment in Spanish class. What is enrollment in French class compared to Spanish class as a fraction and as a percent?

18. Reasoning Write $\frac{9}{12}$ as a decimal and as a percent. Describe two ways to find the answer.

19. Critique Reasoning Sixty percent of the students in Zachary's class ride their bikes to school. Zachary says that $\frac{6}{10}$ of the students ride their bikes to school. Is he right? Explain.

20. Ramon played in 0.7 of his team's basketball games this season. What percent of the games did Ramon play?

21. Nancy recorded 8 movies on her DVR. She watched 5 of the movies. What percent of the movies did Nancy watch?

22. Shelly sold $\frac{8}{25}$ of the total number of raffle tickets for a fundraiser. Write this fraction as a decimal and as a percent.

23. Higher Order Thinking Three classes have the same number of students. The teachers compared attendance on one Friday. Mr. Lopez had 92.5% of his students in class. Mrs. Foster had $\frac{19}{20}$ of her students in class. In Ms. Kelly's class, 0.9 of the students were present. Which teacher had the most students in class that Friday?

☑ Assessment Practice

24. $\frac{7}{25}$ can be represented as a percent. Select all the fractions and decimals that are also equivalent to this percent.

- ☐ $\frac{25}{7}$
- ☐ 0.725
- ☐ $\frac{21}{75}$
- ☐ 0.28
- ☐ $\frac{56}{200}$

25. Out of 232 tourists shopping in Venice, Florida, 25% purchased seashells as souvenirs. Using the percent as a rate per 100, how many tourists purchased seashells?

6-3 Additional Practice

Scan for
Multimedia

In **1–12**, write each percent as a fraction and as a decimal.

1. 137%

2. 115%

3. $\frac{3}{4}$%

4. 0.4%

5. 450%

6. 101%

7. $\frac{9}{25}$%

8. 0.22%

9. 810%

10. $\frac{3}{10}$%

11. 0.25%

12. 0.35%

13. The area of the Simpsons' new house is 150% of the area of their old house. Write this percent as a fraction and as a decimal.

14. The price of a gallon of gas decreased by $\frac{9}{10}$% in one month. How do you express $\frac{9}{10}$% as a fraction and as a decimal?

15. Only 0.6% of the students at a high school did not attend the first football game. Write 0.6% as a fraction and as a decimal.

16. Critique Reasoning Mrs. Kingston's salary is 250% of what it was 20 years ago. She says that her salary is 2.5 times what it was 20 years ago. Is she correct? Explain.

17. Reasoning The interest rate on a credit card increased by $\frac{1}{2}$%. Is $\frac{1}{2}$% less than, equal to, or greater than 0.005? Explain.

18. About 0.45% of the students in Hannah's school have a landline phone at home. How do you express 0.45% as a fraction and as a decimal?

19. Critique Reasoning Jamie said that she could write a decimal percent as a decimal by moving the decimal point two places to the left and deleting the percent sign. Is Jamie correct? How do you know?

20. The distance a salesperson traveled for work this year is 315% of the distance she traveled last year. Write 315% as a fraction and as a decimal.

21. Almost 0.2% of shoppers choose to complete an online survey about their shopping experience. What is 0.2% expressed as a fraction and as a decimal?

22. At the botanical gardens, $\frac{3}{5}$% of the flowers are pink. What is the fraction and decimal equivalent of this percent?

23. Critique Reasoning Roger expressed $\frac{1}{5}$% as $\frac{1}{500}$. Ellen expressed $\frac{1}{5}$% as $\frac{100}{5}$. Who is correct? Explain.

24. Higher Order Thinking Lauren wants to open a savings account. Bank A will increase the interest rate on the savings account by $\frac{1}{4}$% after the first year that Lauren is a customer. Bank B offers an interest rate increase of 0.2% after the first year that she is a customer. Which bank has the higher interest rate increase? Explain.

✓ Assessment Practice

25. Last year, a small manufacturing company netted a profit of $540,000. The net profit increased this year by 135%. What is the net profit of the company this year? Show your work.

26. The image of a plant cell in a science book is enlarged to show the detail of the cell's layers. The actual size of the plant cell is $\frac{1}{8}$% of the picture. Select all of the fractions and decimals that can be expressed as $\frac{1}{8}$%.

☐ $\frac{1}{800}$

☐ 0.00125

☐ 0.125

☐ $\frac{1}{8}$

☐ 1.25

6-4 Additional Practice

Scan for Multimedia

Leveled Practice In **1–9**, estimate the percent of each number.

1. 24% of 94

24% ≈ [   ]

94 ≈ [   ]

[   ] of [   ] = [   ]

2. 54% of 489

54% ≈ [   ]

489 ≈ [   ]

[   ] of [   ] = [   ]

3. 8% of 212

8% ≈ [   ]

212 ≈ [   ]

[   ] of [   ] = [   ]

4. 38% of 102

5. 42% of 300

6. 79% of 13

7. 84% of 900

8. 13% of 97

9. 28% of 90

10. There are 500 sheets of printer paper in a package. Erin uses 18% of the paper when she prints a report for social studies class. About how many sheets of paper does Erin use for her report? Explain.

11. Bob says that he can estimate 72% of 400 using two different fractions. Is he right? Explain.

12. The parking lot at a mall has space for 318 cars. Eight percent of the parking spaces are for compact cars. About how many parking spaces are for compact cars? Explain.

13. The results of a survey of 878 students show that 62% of the students plan to upgrade their smartphones this year. About how many students plan to upgrade? Use compatible numbers to find the answer.

14. The seating capacity at a movie theater is 400. For a Monday afternoon movie, 68% of the seats are filled. About how many seats are empty?

15. Students plant 148 flowers at a community park. Seventy-eight percent of the flowers are pansies. Use rounding to estimate how many flowers are pansies.

16. The Johnson family lives 432 miles from the beach. They drive 52% of the distance before stopping for lunch. About how many miles do they drive before lunch? Explain how you can use mental math to find the answer.

17. **Make Sense and Persevere** Peter bought 34 pumpkins at a farmer's market. He used 27% of the pumpkins to make pumpkin pies. Peter says that he used about 9 pumpkins for pumpkin pies. Explain how Peter estimated.

18. With a full ink cartridge, the printer can print 2,500 pages. The printer cartridge is now 37% full. Estimate the number of pages the printer can still print.

19. **Reasoning** On a rainy day, 76% of the students in the school brought umbrellas. There are 600 students in the school. About how many students brought umbrellas?

20. **Higher Order Thinking** Marcus spent 20% of y dollars to pay for his car to be repaired. What is y if 20% of y is about $40? Explain how you estimated and which property of equality you used to find y.

21. **Make Sense and Persevere** Amanda's dog Zazau ate almost 18% of the 4 dozen cookies that Amanda baked. Estimate the number of cookies Zazau ate.

✓ Assessment Practice

22. The number of students who participate in after-school sports is 180. At an awards ceremony, 15% of the students received an award for sportsmanship and 25% received an award for teamwork.

PART A

Use an equivalent fraction to determine how many students received an award for sportsmanship. Show your work.

PART B

Use an equivalent fraction to determine how many students received an award for teamwork. Show your work.

6-5 Additional Practice

In 1–6, find each part.

1. What is 8% of 200?

2. What is 12% of 800?

3. What is 12.8% of 312.5?

4. What is 46% of 388?

5. What is 86% of 20?

6. What is 4.75% of 2,000?

In 7–12, find each percent.

7. What percent of 186 is 93?

8. What percent of 28 is 7?

9. What percent of 250 is 182?

10. What percent of 88 is 77?

11. What percent of 965 is 193?

12. What percent of 2,160 is 270?

13. Jeb earns $8 per hour. He gets a raise of 3.5%. How much is his raise?

14. On a local sports team, 20% of 50 players are left-handed. How many left-handed players are on the team?

15. Jeff ordered soup and a salad at a restaurant for $7.50. He gave the waitress an 18% tip. Ellen ordered a club sandwich for $8.50. She gave the waitress a 16% tip. Who left the greater tip? How much greater?

16. There are 25 acres of land on a farm. The owners planted corn on 68% of the land. On how many acres did they not plant corn?

In 17–19, use the table.

17. **Reasoning** James has saved $200 to purchase some skateboarding equipment. Can he spend less than 50% of his savings on skateboarding shoes and knee pads? Explain.

Equipment Price List	
Skateboard	$100
Skateboarding Shoes	$60
Knee Pads	$30
Elbow Pads	$20
Wrist Guards	$20
Helmet	$50
Ramp	$115

18. A salesperson suggests that James buy a helmet and a ramp. What percent of his savings would James spend if he bought both items?

19. **Construct Arguments** James has 75% of his savings left. Can he buy a skateboard and shoes? Explain.

20. **Higher Order Thinking** Katrina has a bookcase that holds 200 books. She can put 20 books on each shelf. If 20% of the bookcase is empty, how many shelves are filled with books?

21. **Model with Math** A 50-pound bag of horse feed is a mixture of corn and oats. If 70% of the bag is oats, how many pounds of corn are in a bag? Draw a double number line diagram to show how to find the answer.

Assessment Practice

22. Pamela hired a contractor to paint 75% of the walls in her house. She has 3,996 square feet of walls. How many square feet of the walls are **NOT** painted?

Ⓐ 999 ft²

Ⓑ 2,997 ft²

Ⓒ 3,996 ft²

Ⓓ 6,993 ft²

23. There were 675 people in line for a rock concert. Only 72% of the people got into the concert. How many people did **NOT** get into the concert?

Ⓐ 675 people

Ⓑ 486 people

Ⓒ 297 people

Ⓓ 189 people

6-6 Additional Practice

In 1–8, find each whole.

1. 70% of what number is 35?

2. 300% of what number is 75?

3. 25% of what number is 2?

4. 150% of what number is 48?

5. 0.2% of what number is 8?

6. 50% of what number is 15?

7. 300% of what number is 51?

8. 37.5% of what number is 6?

9. Kelly had a part-time job last year. She paid the state $234 in income tax. The state income tax rate is 5.2%. How much did Kelly earn?

10. Donations of $375 in March to a homeless shelter are 250% of what they were in February. What were donations to the shelter in February?

11. The number of visitors to a sporting goods website is 1,940 today. This is 400% of the number of visitors on the first day the site was online. How many visitors did the website have on the first day?

12. Reasoning Horatio recorded the daily high temperatures. On 66 days, the high temperature was greater than 88°F. This was 75% of the days that Horatio recorded. How many days was the high temperature less than or equal to 88°F?

13. Maria sold 50 books, or 40% of her book collection, at a yard sale. How many books were in Maria's collection?

14. Reasoning Sam and his friends had take-out spaghetti and meatballs for dinner. The tax was $3. The tax rate is 7.5%. What was the price of the dinners including tax?

In 15 and 16, use the art at the right.

15. A medium artichoke contains about 13% of the recommended amount of potassium that an average adult should have each day. About how many grams of potassium should the average adult have each day?

A medium artichoke contains about 0.474 g of potassium.

16. **Reasoning** A medium artichoke contains about 7 grams of dietary fiber. This is about 28% of the recommended dietary fiber that an average adult should eat each day. About how many artichokes would an average adult have to eat to get the recommended daily amount of dietary fiber?

17. **Higher Order Thinking** An electronics store sold 4% of the computers that were on sale. If only 12 computers were sold, how many computers were not sold? Write an equation to solve.

18. The number of students in a band that play guitar is 2, or 20% of the students in the band. How many students are in the band?

19. **Critique Reasoning** The number of students who signed a petition for more after-school sports is 195, or 30% of the students at school. Terry's calculations show that there are 58.5 students, but he knows that number is incorrect. What is the correct enrollment? What was Terry's error?

20. Helen and Carla live in states that have different sales tax rates. They each bought a new bicycle. Helen paid $14 for a 5.6% sales tax on her bicycle. Carla paid $12 for a 4.8% sales tax on her bicycle. Who paid more for their bicycle, not including sales tax? Explain.

✓ Assessment Practice

21. The cost for a 5-day business trip for 3 people is $1,975 per person. The business trip would use 79% of the company's travel budget. Find the total amount of money the company has budgeted for travel. Show your work.

22. The amount of time Jill trained for a marathon this month is 125% of the amount of time she trained last month. If Jill trained for 80 hours last month, how many hours did she train this month?

7-1 Additional Practice

In 1–6, find the area of each parallelogram or rhombus.

1.

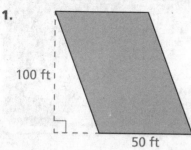

100 ft

50 ft

2.

7 m

12 m

3.

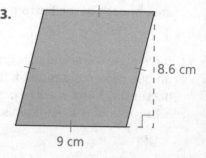

8.6 cm

9 cm

4. Rhombus

$b = 30$ m

$h = 15.5$ m

5. Parallelogram

$b = 18$ in.

$h = 2\frac{1}{2}$ in.

6. Parallelogram

$b = 20$ ft

$h = 3$ yd

7. The area of the parallelogram is 105 cm². What is the base of the parallelogram?

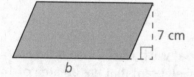

7 cm

b

8. The area of the rhombus is 216 in.². What is the height of the rhombus?

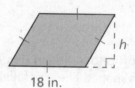

h

18 in.

9. Benjamin's garden is shaped like a rhombus. The area of his garden is 336 square feet. The height of the rhombus that represents his garden is 16 feet. What is the base of the rhombus?

10. A rhombus has a base of 5.2 meters and a height of 4.5 meters. The rhombus is divided into two identical triangles. What is the area of each triangle?

11. Sarah applies the pearl guitar fret markers to her fret board as shown. Each fret marker is in the shape of a parallelogram. Each of the three bottom fret markers has a base that measures 52.5 mm and a height of 6 mm. What is the area of each of the bottom fret markers?

12. **Be Precise** A rectangular guitar case has a unique rhombus design on the top that has a height of 13 inches and a base of 2 feet. What is the area of the design in square inches?

13. **Higher Order Thinking** Tony says that he does not have enough information to find the area of this parallelogram. Is he correct? Explain.

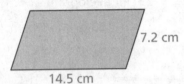

7.2 cm

14.5 cm

14. Rhombus A has a base of 7 inches and an area of 35 square inches. Rhombus B has a base and height that are three times the base and height of rhombus A. Find the area of rhombus B and compare it to the area of rhombus A. Explain.

15. A modern office building in Hamburg, Germany, is shaped like a parallelogram. The front of the building has a base of 123 meters and a height of 23 meters. What is the area of the front of the building?

16. **Model with Math** Dan drew a parallelogram that has an area of 144 square inches to represent a section of sidewalk. Draw an example of the parallelogram that Dan could have drawn.

✅ Assessment Practice

17. Find the area of the given parallelogram using two different methods. Justify your answer.

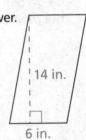

14 in.

6 in.

Name: _____

7-2 Additional Practice

In 1–9, find the area of each triangle.

1.

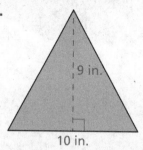

9 in.

10 in.

2.

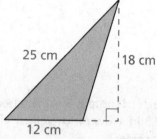

25 cm

18 cm

12 cm

3.

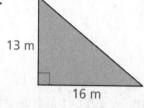

13 m

16 m

4. Triangle

$b = 30$ m

$h = 15.6$ m

5. Triangle

$b = 18$ in.

$h = 6\frac{1}{2}$ in.

6. Triangle

$b = 8$ yd

$h = 3$ yd

7. Triangle

$b = 11$ ft

$h = 7$ ft

8. Triangle

$b = 200$ cm

$h = 100$ cm

9. Triangle

$b = 14.2$ in.

$h = 7$ in.

10. Pedro is building a playground in the shape of a right triangle. He wants to know the area of the playground to decide how much sand to buy. What is the area of the playground?

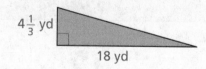

$4\frac{1}{3}$ yd

18 yd

11. The dimensions of a clock face are shown below. Find the area of the clock face.

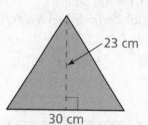

23 cm

30 cm

12. **Be Precise** The base of a triangle is 4.4 m. The height of the triangle is 250 cm. What is the area of the triangle in square meters?

13. The vertices of a triangle are $A(4, 1)$, $B(9, 1)$, and $C(2, 5)$. What is the area of this triangle?

In 14 and 15, use the diagram at the right.

14. **Make Sense and Persevere** A gymnastics incline mat is shaped like a wedge. Two sides of the mat are shaped like right triangles. How much vinyl is needed to cover both of the triangular sides?

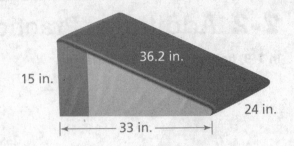

15 in.

36.2 in.

24 in.

33 in.

15. The width of the blue vinyl in each triangle is 6 in. The height of the yellow right triangle is 12.3 in. How much yellow vinyl is needed for each of the triangular sides?

16. **Higher Order Thinking** The area of a triangle is 36 cm². Give three possible sets of dimensions for the triangle's base and height, and explain whether you can also give the side lengths of the triangle.

17. **Be Precise** A triangle has a base of 2 m and a height of 4 m. Find the area of the triangle in square millimeters.

18. Triangle *GHK* has an area of 117 cm². Write and solve an equation to find the height, *h*, of triangle *GHK*.

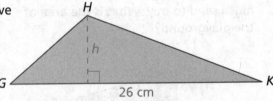

H

h

G

26 cm

K

19. Select all of the equations that represent the area of the given triangle.

☐ $A = 15 \times 20$

☐ $A = \frac{1}{2}(15 \times 20)$

☐ $A = 12 \times 20$

☐ $A = \frac{1}{2}(25 \times 12)$

☐ $A = \frac{1}{2}(20 \times 12)$

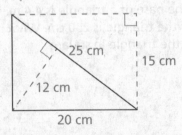

25 cm

15 cm

12 cm

20 cm

Name: _____

7-3 Additional Practice

In **1–6**, find the area of each trapezoid or kite.

1.

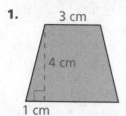

3 cm

4 cm

1 cm

5 cm

2.

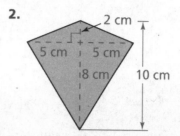

2 cm

5 cm 5 cm

8 cm

10 cm

3.

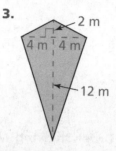

2 m

4 m 4 m

12 m

4.

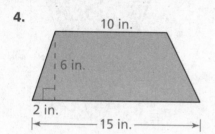

10 in.

6 in.

2 in.

15 in.

5.

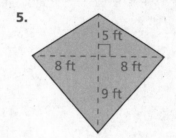

5 ft

8 ft 8 ft

9 ft

6.

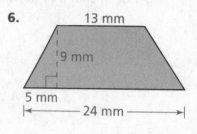

13 mm

9 mm

5 mm

24 mm

7. A desktop has the shape of a trapezoid. What is the area of the desktop?

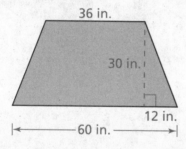

36 in.

30 in.

12 in.

60 in.

8. Kelsey cut pieces of fabric in the shape of kites for a quilt. One piece is shown below. What is the area of the piece of fabric?

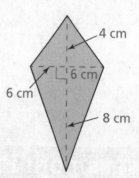

4 cm

6 cm

6 cm

8 cm

9. The area of the kite is 28 m². What is the value of x?

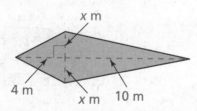

x m

4 m

x m 10 m

10. What is the area of the trapezoid below?

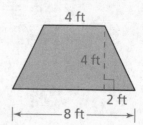

4 ft

4 ft

2 ft

8 ft

11. Construct Arguments Joshua is taking this kite to the Zilker Kite Festival. He wants to know its area to see whether he has a chance of winning the largest kite contest. Does Joshua have enough information to find the area of the kite? Explain.

Joshua's Kite

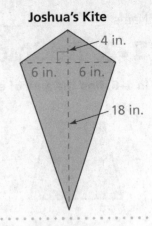

12. Higher Order Thinking Mia has the kite shown. Without calculating the area, how can you tell whether Mia's kite is larger or smaller than Joshua's kite in Exercise 11? Explain.

Mia's Kite

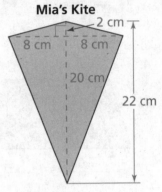

13. Reasoning Ben says that the area of the triangle at the right equals the area of the trapezoid. If Ben's statement is true, what is the height, *h*, of the triangle? Explain.

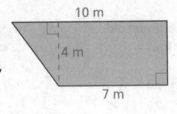
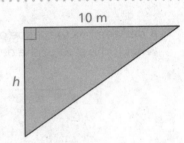

Assessment Practice

14. Haley is drawing the design of the awning shown below. The two triangular sections are identical isosceles right triangles. She needs to find the total area of the awning. Find the area of the awning by decomposing the trapezoid into familiar shapes.

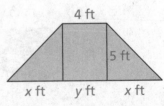

7-4 Additional Practice

In 1–4, find the area of each polygon or shaded region.

1.

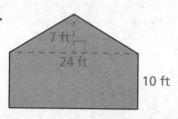

7 ft
24 ft
10 ft

2.

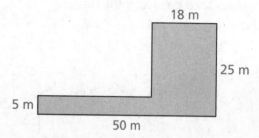

18 m
25 m
5 m
50 m

3.

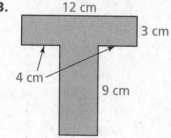

12 cm
3 cm
4 cm
9 cm

4.

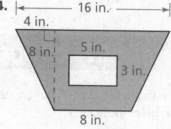

16 in.
4 in.
8 in.
5 in.
3 in.
8 in.

In 5 and 6, find the area of each polygon in square units.

5.

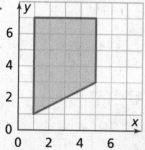

6.

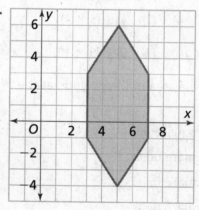

7. The city engineer plans to insert a storm water drain within a public garden space. The green garden space will be filled with rocks and plants that help to purify the water. What is the area of the space that will be filled with plants and rocks?

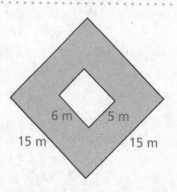

6 m
5 m
15 m
15 m

8. **Higher Order Thinking** Mrs. Via needs to buy grass seed for her yard. She drew a diagram of her yard. Each square represents 1 square yard. Five pounds of seed is enough to plant 100 square yards of grass. Grass seed is sold in 2-pound bags. How many bags of grass seed does Mrs. Via need?

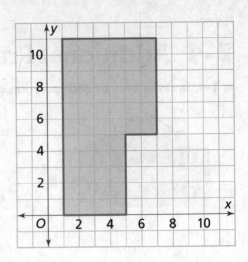

9. Select all of the expressions that can be used to find the area of the given polygon.

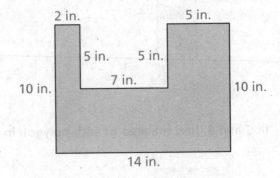

☐ $(10 \times 14) - (7 \times 5)$

☐ $(2 \times 10) + (5 \times 10) + (14 \times 10)$

☐ $(6 \times 14) + (2 \times 10) + (5 \times 10)$

☐ $(10 \times 4) + (2 \times 4) + (5 \times 4)$

☐ $(2 \times 10) + (7 \times 5) + (5 \times 10)$

10. What is the area of the polygon at the right?

Ⓐ 161.5 square units

Ⓑ 164 square units

Ⓒ 170 square units

Ⓓ 182 square units

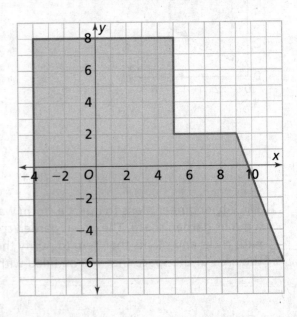

7-5 Additional Practice

In 1–3, classify the solid figures.

1.

2.

3.

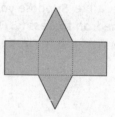

In 4–6, identify each solid from its net.

4.

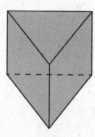

5.

6.

7. Josh is going to draw a net of a triangular prism. How many rectangles should there be in his drawing?

8. Monique is going to draw a net of a triangular pyramid. How many triangles should there be in her drawing?

9. Draw a net of a rectangular prism that has bases that are 2 units long and 2 units wide and a height of 3 units.

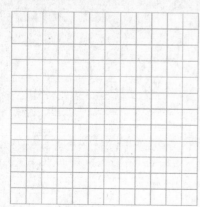

10. **Critique Reasoning** Eli drew this net for a triangular prism. Explain why Eli's net is not correct.

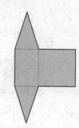

11. Classify the polyhedron. Name all of the vertices, edges, and faces.

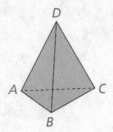

12. Higher Order Thinking If the top of a pencil box is 8 inches by 3 inches and the side is 3 inches by 2 inches, can you find the dimensions of the front of the box? Explain.

13. Generalize Suppose you are shown a polyhedron to classify. Describe the process you would use to classify it.

14. Marguerite draws a net of a solid figure. The net has 1 square face and 4 triangular faces. For which polyhedron did Marguerite draw a net?

15. Use Structure A solid may have several nets. The net at the right can be folded to make a solid. Identify the solid it forms. Then draw a different net of that solid.

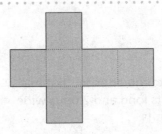

16. A square pyramid is 4 units long and the height of each triangular face is 3 units. Draw a net that represents this pyramid.

7-6 Additional Practice

Scan for
Multimedia

In **1–6**, find the surface area of each prism.

1.

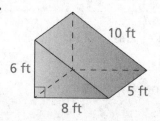

10 ft
6 ft
5 ft
8 ft

2.

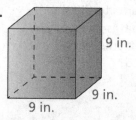

9 in.
9 in.
9 in.

3.

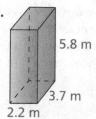

5.8 m
3.7 m
2.2 m

4.

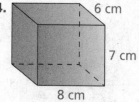

6 cm
7 cm
8 cm

5.

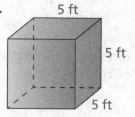

5 ft
5 ft
5 ft

6.

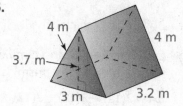

4 m
4 m
3.7 m
3 m
3.2 m

---

7. A factory produces cube-shaped boxes like the figure shown. Find the surface area of one box.

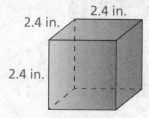

2.4 in.
2.4 in.
2.4 in.

8. Make Sense and Persevere The triangular faces of the prism shown are equilateral triangles with a perimeter of 48 cm. Each of the other faces is a square. Find the surface area of the prism.

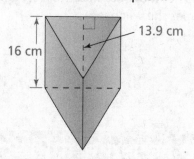

16 cm
13.9 cm

---

9. Ayasha and Michael draw cubes. Each side of Ayasha's cube has a length of 7 m. Each side of Michael's cube has a length that is double the length of Ayasha's cube. Compare the surface areas of the cubes.

10. Be Precise A box is shaped like a rectangular prism. The length is $1\frac{1}{4}$ ft, the width is 8 in., and the height is 10 in. Find the surface area of the box in square inches.

In 11–14, use the table.

11. Fill in the area of each color tile.

Color	Tile Size	Area
Black	4 in. × 4 in.	
Red	2 in. × 2 in.	
Green	8 in. × 8 in.	

12. Make Sense and Persevere Mora wants to tile the surface of a rectangular storage case that is 24 inches long, 16 inches wide, and 8 inches tall. If she uses all green tiles, how many tiles will she need?

13. If Mora uses all black tiles, how many tiles will she need?

14. Mora has another storage case that is a cube. The length of each side is 18 inches. If she uses all red tiles to tile the case, how many tiles will she need?

15. Critique Reasoning Emilio used the expression shown to find the surface area of the prism. Is his expression correct? Explain.

$SA = 2(12) + 2(18) + 2(12)$

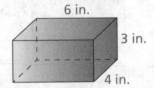
6 in.
3 in.
4 in.

16. Higher Order Thinking Alexa draws and labels the diagram to represent the file organizers shown. She wants to cover the outside and bottom of the organizers with decorative paper. Explain how she can use her model to find the least amount of paper she will need.

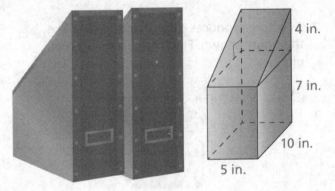
4 in.
7 in.
10 in.
5 in.

17. Using a net, find the surface area, in square meters, of a rectangular prism with a length of 2.8 meters, width of 4.3 meters, and a height of 6.2 meters?

18. The surface area of a cube is 71.415 square feet. The net of the prism is shown. What are the possible dimensions of the cube in feet?

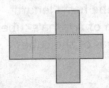

Ⓐ 3, 3, 3   Ⓒ 3.45, 3.45, 3.45

Ⓑ 3, 3.45, 3.45   Ⓓ 3.5, 3.5, 3.5

7-7 Additional Practice

In 1 and 2, find the surface area of each pyramid by drawing its net. The faces of the triangular pyramid are equilateral triangles.

1.

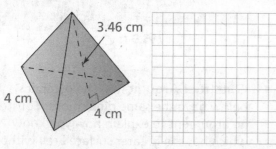

3.46 cm

4 cm

4 cm

2.

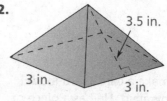

3.5 in.

3 in.   3 in.

In 3–6, find the surface area of each pyramid. The faces of the triangular pyramid are equilateral triangles.

3.

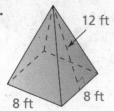

12 ft

8 ft   8 ft

4.

7.8 cm

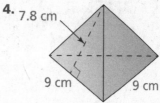

9 cm   9 cm

5.

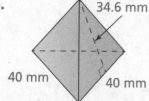

34.6 mm

40 mm   40 mm

6.

15 in.

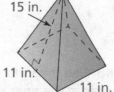

11 in.   11 in.

7. The base of a square pyramid has side lengths of 4.8 m. The height of each triangular face of the pyramid is 6 m. Do you have enough information to find the surface area of the pyramid? Explain.

8. The area of the base of a triangular pyramid with faces that are equilateral triangles is 64 ft². Can you find the surface area of the pyramid? Explain.

9. The Great Pyramid of Giza in Egypt is a square pyramid. What some scientists believe to be the original dimensions of the pyramid are shown at the right. What is the surface area of this famous pyramid?

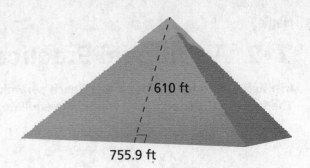

610 ft

755.9 ft

10. Rico wants to make a cardboard model of this square pyramid. He has a piece of cardboard that is 20 in. long and 18 in. wide. Does he have enough cardboard for the model? Explain.

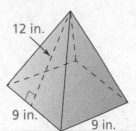

12 in.

9 in.

9 in.

11. **Construct Arguments** The pyramids below have the same dimensions. Construct an argument to explain how you know which has the greater surface area without calculating.

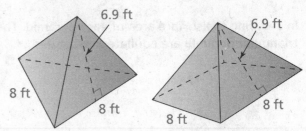

6.9 ft

6.9 ft

8 ft

8 ft

8 ft

8 ft

12. **Higher Order Thinking** Find the surface area of the rectangular pyramid at the right.

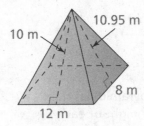

10 m

10.95 m

8 m

12 m

Assessment Practice

13. Which net represents the pyramid with the greatest surface area?

Ⓐ
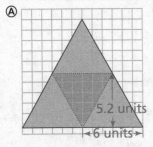

5.2 units

6 units

Ⓑ
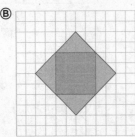

Ⓒ
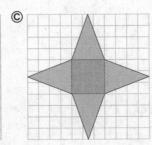

Ⓓ
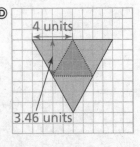

4 units

3.46 units

7-8 Additional Practice

Scan for Multimedia

In 1–9, find the volume of each rectangular prism.

1.

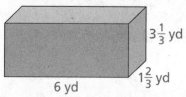

$3\frac{1}{3}$ yd

$1\frac{2}{3}$ yd

6 yd

2.

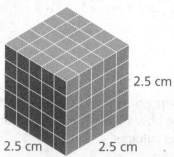

2.5 cm

2.5 cm   2.5 cm

3.

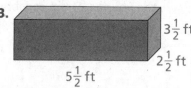

$3\frac{1}{2}$ ft

$2\frac{1}{2}$ ft

$5\frac{1}{2}$ ft

4.

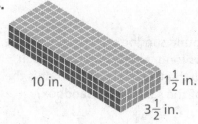

10 in.

$1\frac{1}{2}$ in.

$3\frac{1}{2}$ in.

5.

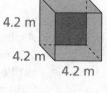

4.2 m

4.2 m

4.2 m

6.

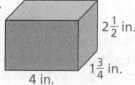

$2\frac{1}{2}$ in.

$1\frac{3}{4}$ in.

4 in.

7. length = $5\frac{1}{4}$ in.

width = $3\frac{3}{4}$ in.

height = 2 in.

8. length = 1.5 m

width = 0.75 m

height = 1.4 m

9. length = $3\frac{1}{2}$ yd

width = $3\frac{1}{2}$ yd

height = $3\frac{1}{2}$ yd

10. Reasoning Without calculating, Steven says that prisms A and B have the same volume. Explain why Steven is correct.

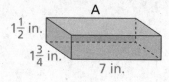

A

$1\frac{1}{2}$ in.

$1\frac{3}{4}$ in.

7 in.

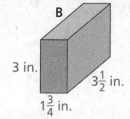

B

3 in.

$3\frac{1}{2}$ in.

$1\frac{3}{4}$ in.

11. Write an equation that you can use to find the volume of the cube. Then find the volume.

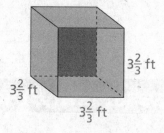

$3\frac{2}{3}$ ft

$3\frac{2}{3}$ ft

$3\frac{2}{3}$ ft

In **12 and 13**, use the diagram at the right.

12. **Make Sense and Persevere** Marita uses the pan for cornbread. There is $\frac{3}{4}$ inch of space left at the top of the pan when her cornbread is done baking. What is the volume of the cornbread Marita made?

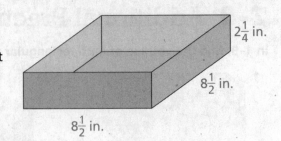

$2\frac{1}{4}$ in.

$8\frac{1}{2}$ in.

$8\frac{1}{2}$ in.

13. **Model with Math** When Marita pours the cornbread batter into the pan, the pan is half full. Explain how you can find the volume of the batter in the pan. Then find the volume.

14. **Be Precise** A toy box is shaped like a cube with each edge 1.2 meters long. Find the volume of the toy box in cubic meters and in cubic centimeters. How many cubic centimeters are in 1 cubic meter?

15. A playground sandbox is 3.5 meters wide, 2.5 meters long, and 0.3 meter deep. It is filled to the top with sand. What is the volume of the sand in the sandbox?

16. **Higher Order Thinking** Find the volumes of the two rectangular prisms described in the table. If you divide each dimension of the larger prism by 2, how does the new volume compare to its original volume? Explain.

Length	Width	Height	Volume
5 in.	$4\frac{1}{2}$ in.	6 in.	
$2\frac{1}{2}$ in.	$2\frac{1}{4}$ in.	3 in.	

17. Which rectangular prism with the given dimensions has the same volume as the prism shown?

  Ⓐ $\frac{1}{2}$ ft, $2\frac{3}{4}$ ft, 7 ft   Ⓒ 1 ft, $2\frac{3}{4}$ ft, 7 ft

  Ⓑ 1 ft, $2\frac{3}{4}$ ft, $3\frac{1}{2}$ ft   Ⓓ $1\frac{1}{2}$ ft, 3 ft, $5\frac{1}{2}$ ft

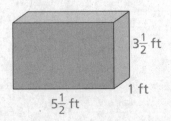

$3\frac{1}{2}$ ft

1 ft

$5\frac{1}{2}$ ft

8-1 Additional Practice

In 1 and 2, determine whether each question is *statistical* or *not statistical*.

1. How long does it take sixth-grade students to eat lunch?

2. When does Carver Elementary School's summer break begin?

3. Write a statistical question that you might ask to gather data on the cost of a restaurant meal.

4. Write a statistical question that you might ask to gather information about the recycling habits of your neighbors.

5. Tiana asked her classmates, "Will you take Chorus or Music Appreciation next semester?" She collected these responses: 11 classmates chose Chorus and 17 chose Music Appreciation. Make a frequency table to display these data.

6. Dean asked his classmates, "How many apples did you eat last week?" He got the following responses: 7, 5, 5, 5, 7, 3, 2, 1, 0, 0, 4, 3, 2, 1, 0, 7, 5, 6, 7, 0, 2, 2, 1, 4. Make a dot plot to display the data.

7. Why is the following a statistical question? Explain.

   In which months were the students in the class born?

8. Is the following question statistical? Explain.

   How many hours did your friend spend online last night?

In 9–11, use the bar graph at the right.

9. **Make Sense and Persevere** What statistical question might Tessa have asked her classmates to gather the data displayed in the bar graph?

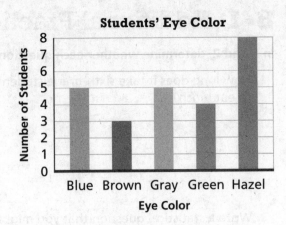

10. **Higher Order Thinking** People with *heterochromia* have two different-colored eyes. A new student in Tessa's class has heterochromia. How might you show that the student has one blue eye and one brown eye on the bar graph? Explain.

11. **Be Precise** Could Tessa represent these data using a dot plot? Explain.

Assessment Practice

12. Charles asked each member of the basketball team these two questions:

   - *How many inches tall are you?*
   - *How many points were scored in the last game?*

   Which of the questions that Charles asked is a statistical question? Explain.

13. Select all of the statistical questions.

   ☐ In a typical week, how many minutes do you spend exercising?

   ☐ What is your favorite magazine?

   ☐ How many nickels are in one dollar?

   ☐ Which U.S. state has the largest population?

   ☐ Does MacKenzie wear glasses?

Name: _____

8-2 Additional Practice

Scan for
Multimedia

In 1 and 2, find the mean of the data given.

1. Number of pets in six families: 3, 0, 2, 4, 2, 1

2. Number of apps on five friends' smart phones: 42, 42, 23, 75, 64

In 3–7, use the data table.

3. Order the data from least to greatest.

4. What are the median and the mode of the data?

5. How do you find the range of the data? What is the range of this data set?

6. Use Structure A newspaper wanted to summarize the data without including Alaska and Hawaii. How does this affect the median?

7. Look for Relationships How does deleting the data for Alaska and Hawaii affect the mode and the range?

National Parks in Western States	
Alaska	23
Arizona	22
California	26
Colorado	13
Hawaii	7
Idaho	6
Montana	8
Nevada	3
New Mexico	13
Oregon	6
Utah	13
Washington	13
Wyoming	7

In 8 and 9, use the data about the weekly salaries of employees at two small companies.

Company A: $500, $510, $530, $510, $550
Company B: $450, $440, $440, $470, $800

8. What is the mean weekly salary at each company?

9. Generalize Four of the five employees at Company B each received a raise of $40. After the raises, how much greater is the mean of the salaries for Company B than for Company A? Explain how you solved the problem.

In 10–12, use the data listed at the right.

10. What is the median? How do you find the median of this set of data?

Long Jump Distances at Parker Middle School Track Meet (m)
5.46, 5.92, 2.95, 5.06, 4.1, 5.45, 5.07, 5.06, 5.9

11. What are the mode and the range of the data?

12. **Look for Relationships** If a tenth competitor were to jump 1.01 meters, which measure would change the most: the median, the mode, or the range? Explain.

In 13–15, use the data listed at the right.

13. Some band members have raised much more money than others. Which measure can be used to show this? Explain.

Money Each Student Has Raised for a Band Trip
$24.50, $18.25, $5.75, $48.00, $32.50, $12.80, $22.90, $35.00, $18.75, $16.25

14. What is the mean amount raised by the students?

15. **Higher Order Thinking** How much more money do the 10 students need to raise to increase the mean to $25.00? Explain.

✓ Assessment Practice

16. The number of historic landmarks in different southern states is shown in the data table. The state of Kentucky, which has 30 historic landmarks, is now added to this data set. Select all of the statements that are true.

National Historic Landmarks in Southern States	
Alabama	37
Florida	43
Georgia	48
Louisiana	53
Mississippi	39
Tennessee	30

☐ The mean of the data will decrease.

☐ The range of the data will decrease.

☐ The mean of the data will stay the same.

☐ The range of the data will stay the same.

☐ The mean of the data will increase.

Name: _____

8-3 Additional Practice

1. In a bowling tournament, Sofia got the following scores:
167, 178, 193, 196, 199, 199, 203, 209, 217, 220, 221.

   a. What is the median?

   b. What is the first quartile?

   c. What is the third quartile?

   d. Draw a box plot of the data.

   e. Write two conclusions about the data shown in the box plot.

2. Sabrina grows flowers. In a competition with other flower growers, she earned the following scores: 7, 10, 10, 6, 7, 8, 8, 7, 9.

   a. What is the median?

   b. What is the first quartile?

   c. What is the third quartile?

   d. Draw a box plot of the data.

   e. Write two conclusions about the data shown in the box plot.

In 3 and 4, use this data set, which shows how many miles Tisha ran each week for 10 weeks.
4, 9, 8, 6, 14, 11, 14, 8, 16, 12

3. Find the statistical measures that you need to make a box plot of Tisha's running distances.

4. Make a box plot to represent Tisha's running distances.

In 5 and 6, use this data set, which shows the prices, in dollars, of 10 coats.
55, 75, 45, 80, 50, 70, 45, 85, 60, 70

5. Find the statistical measures you need to make a box plot of the coat prices.

6. Make a box plot to display the coat prices.

In 7 and 8, draw box plots using the data provided.

7. The sizes of different computer files, in megabytes:

   114, 134, 191, 216, 255, 181, 189

8. The rainfall, in inches per year, for seven different states:

   83, 57, 48, 97, 20, 36, 31

In 9 and 10, use the box plot to answer the question.

9. How much does the less expensive 50% of trail mix cost?

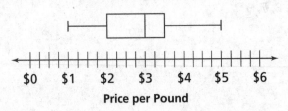

Costs of Trail Mix

Price per Pound

10. How much does the most expensive sandwich cost?

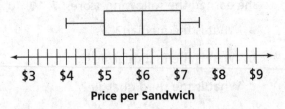

Costs of Sandwiches

Price per Sandwich

---

11. **Higher Order Thinking** Terence made a box plot showing the number of points scored at football games. Without seeing the values, what part of the scores fall in the range represented by the box? Explain.

12. **Critique Reasoning** Casey recorded the weights, in pounds, of 10 cats at the vet's office: 5, 8, 6, 13, 16, 12, 5, 8, 10, 15. Casey then drew a box plot using the weights. What error did Casey make?

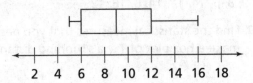

---

13. Use the given data to complete the box plot.

   Shantay tossed a pair of number cubes numbered 1–6 a total of 10 times. The sums of the numbers on her cubes for each of her tosses are shown in the table.

Sum of Pair of Tossed Number Cubes
11 3 9 5 10 7 7 6 7 6

   Complete the box plot to show the distribution of the sums.

   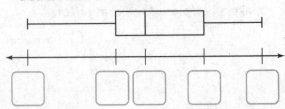

8-4 Additional Practice

Scan for
Multimedia

In 1 and 2, use the data in the chart.

Annual Ticket Sales for Charity Ice-Skating Event							
72	81	88	51	90	89	85	74
87	100	80	99	87	96	99	84
84	86	94	88	91	85	78	90

1. Complete the frequency table below for the number of tickets sold each year for the charity event.

Tickets Sold	Tallies	Frequency
45–54		
55–64		
65–74		
75–84		
85–94		
95–104		

2. Use your frequency table to complete the histogram.

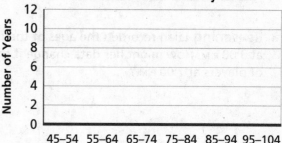

Tickets Sold for Charity Event

In 3–6, use the data in the frequency table. The frequency table shows the time it took students in a P.E. class to run 1 mile.

3. How many students are in the P.E. class?

Time in Minutes	Tally	Frequency
8:00–8:59	‖‖ I	6
9:00–9:59	‖	2
10:00–10:59	‖‖ ‖‖	8
11:00–11:59	‖‖ I	6
12:00–12:59	‖‖ ‖‖‖	9

4. How many students ran 1 mile in under 9 minutes?

5. How many fewer students ran 1 mile in under 10 minutes than students who took 11 or more minutes to run that distance?

6. Be Precise Can you tell from the frequency table how many students, if any, ran a mile in exactly 12 minutes? Explain.

In 7–9, use the chart below and the histogram at the right.

Ages of Players at Castle Miniature Golf				
14	7	6	24	15
9	19	25	10	17
51	8	21	48	12

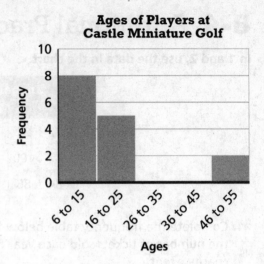

7. Just as Lilah finished making her histogram, a group of five people started playing. She wants to include their ages, which are 12, 12, 16, 26, and 48. How should Lilah change her histogram to include these ages?

8. **Reasoning** Lilah recorded the ages of the miniature golf players at 3:00 P.M. How might her data change if she recorded the ages of players at 7:00 P.M.?

9. **Higher Order Thinking** Suppose a 65-year-old brings her two granddaughters to play miniature golf. The granddaughters are both 5 years old. How can Lilah adjust the intervals to include these ages?

✓ Assessment Practice

10. Use the data given to complete the histogram.

Each day for a month, Bo timed himself to see how many free throws he could make in 60 seconds and recorded the results.

0, 1, 1, 2, 3, 4, 5, 6, 6, 7, 7, 8, 8, 9, 10, 10, 11, 11, 11, 11, 12, 12, 13, 13, 14, 15, 16, 16, 18, 19, 22

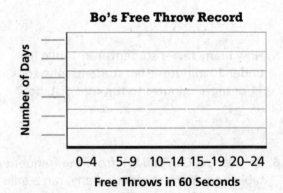

8-5 Additional Practice

In **1** and **2**, complete the tables to find the MAD of each data set.

1.

Data Value	Absolute Deviation
10	$|25 - 10| =$
15	
20	
30	
50	
MAD =	

2.

Data Value	Absolute Deviation
126	
138	
276	
178	
236	
90	
MAD =	

In **3** and **4**, find the range and the IQR for the data in each table.

3. Find the range and the IQR for the data in Exercise 1.

4. Find the range and the IQR for the data in Exercise 2.

In **5** and **6**, use the data shown in the box plot.

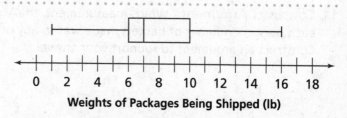

Weights of Packages Being Shipped (lb)

5. What are the range and the IQR?

6. Describe the variability of the data.

In **7** and **8**, use the data shown in the dot plot.

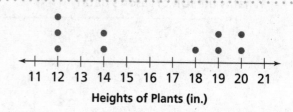

Heights of Plants (in.)

7. What are the mean and the MAD?

8. Describe the variability of the data.

In 9–13, use the data in the table.

9. At a carnival booth, people pay $1 to take 5 free throws. They win a prize based on the number of baskets they make. Vera recorded the number of baskets 20 people made out of 5 shots in the table. Complete the frequency table.

Number of Baskets Made	Tallies	Frequency
0	|||	
1	||||	
2	ⅢⅡ	
3	|||	
4	|||	
5	||	

10. **Higher Order Thinking** Without making the calculations, what do you expect the MAD to be? Explain.

11. **Reasoning** Vera needs to find the mean number of baskets made to find the MAD. How can you find the mean of the tallied data?

12. What is the MAD of Vera's data? What is the IQR?

13. **Construct Arguments** Which measurement, the MAD or the IQR, describes how close each person's number of baskets made was to any other person's number of baskets made? Construct an argument to support your answer.

☑ Assessment Practice

14. Jason recorded the number of hours of sunshine each day for 7 days as shown in the table.

Hours of Sunshine

12, 10, 3, 8, 13, 11, 5

PART A

What is the IQR of Jason's data?

PART B

Select all the statements that best describe the IQR, MAD, and variability of the data set.

☐ The MAD shows that the number of hours of sunshine does not vary greatly from the mean.

☐ The MAD is less than the IQR.

☐ 50% of the days have between 5 and 12 hours of sunshine.

☐ The MAD is greater than the IQR.

☐ The hours of sunshine vary about 3 hours from the mean.

8-6 Additional Practice

Scan for Multimedia

In 1–4, use the data table.

Cost of Kick Scooters at Ted's Sports							
$125	$135	$130	$140	$135	$154	$135	$130

1. Make a dot plot of these data.

2. What are the mean, median, and mode of these prices? Which measure best describes the center of these data? Explain.

3. Which measure would you use to describe the variability of these data? Explain.

4. Describe the center and variability of these prices.

In 5–7, use the dot plot. The dot plot shows the ages of soloists in an orchestra.

Ages of Soloists

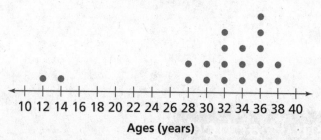

Ages (years)

5. a. Is the mean, median, or mode the best measure of center for these data? Explain.

6. Identify a good measure of variability for these data. Find the value.

b. Find that measure of center.

7. Write a sentence describing the variability of the ages of the soloists.

In 8–10, use the data below.

8. **Model with Math** Make a dot plot for the data.

9 Game Scores		
50	60	80
65	50	55
65	70	50

9. What are the mean, median, and mode of the data, rounded to the nearest whole number? Are there any outliers?

10. **Generalize** Use what you know about statistical measures to explain which measure of center best describes the data set.

In 11 and 12, use the data table.

Cost of 6 Brands of Shampoo					
$1	$2	$4	$6	$7	$20

11. What is the outlier in this data set?

12. **Reasoning** Does an outlier affect the IQR? Does an outlier affect the MAD? Explain.

☑ Assessment Practice

13. The table shows the number of home runs hit by eight baseball players last season. Select the statements that best describe the data.

Home Runs Hit			
42	31	35	17
43	42	53	57

☐ There are outliers in the data set.

☐ The mean best describes the center.

☐ The MAD best describes the variability.

☐ The IQR best describes the spread.

☐ The MAD is 9.25 home runs and the IQR is 15 home runs.

8-7 Additional Practice

Scan for
Multimedia

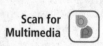

In 1–4, use the data in the box plot.

1. Find the median for the data. What does the median indicate about the data in this problem?

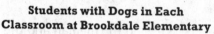

Students with Dogs in Each Classroom at Brookdale Elementary

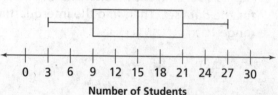

2. What is the interquartile range?

3. Describe the shape of the data distribution.

4. If a dot plot were used to display the same data, what would it look like?

---

5. Be Precise The 25 students in a math class took turns flipping a coin 20 times. The dot plot shows the number of times the result was heads.

Results of Coin Tosses

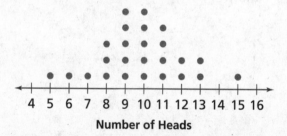

Number of Heads

a. What do any clusters and gaps in the dot plot tell you about the likelihood of the coin landing on heads?

b. Which measures, if any, would be best to summarize the data?

6. Use Structure The school nurse asked 15 parents how many hours they spend exercising each week. The dot plot displays the data.

Hours Exercising per Week

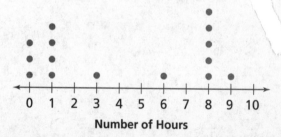

Number of Hours

a. What do any clusters and gaps in the dot plot tell you about the exercise habits of the parents?

b. Which measures, if any, would be best to summarize the data?

In 7–11, use the data to answer the questions.

Lengths of Long Jumps in Mr. Hansen's Physical Education Class (in inches)
91, 72, 76, 77, 79, 79, 76, 72, 80, 83, 85, 89, 76, 80, 79, 82, 84, 80

7. **Be Precise** Find the median and the mean for the data set. Then find the interquartile range.

8. What would be the preferable measure of center, the median or the mean? Explain your reasoning.

9. **Model with Math** Complete a box plot and a dot plot for the data.

10. **Higher Order Thinking** Describe the shape of the data distributions. Explain how the dot plot and the box plot are similar and different.

11. **Use Structure** Matt says that the mean would be more affected than the median if a long jump of 110 inches were added to the data. Do you agree? Explain how you know.

12. Which statement about the pet fish data is true?

   Ⓐ The median and the mean are the same.

   Ⓑ A good representation for the center of the data is 2.

   Ⓒ The data are symmetrical.

   Ⓓ The data show that most students have 3 or more fish.

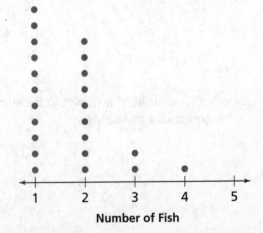

Number of Pet Fish Students Own

Number of Fish